EPIPHANY

A Journey of Self-Discovery

GIOVANNA BURGESS GEATHERS, MA, LPC, LPCS

Giovanna Burgess Geathers
Epiphany: A Journey of Self-Discovery
Edited by: Jessie
Cover Design: Zona Graphics/Zunaira Saleem
Published by: Giovanna Burgess Geathers, LLC Simpsonville, SC 29680

ISBN: 978-0-578-76766-6

Library of Congress Control Number: 2020919222

Printed in the United States of America
10 9 8 7 6 5 4 3 2 1

Note: This book is intended for use as an informational guide only. The reader assumes all responsibility for the consequences of any actions taken based on the information presented in this book. Although the author and publisher have made every effort to ensure that the information in this book was accurate at the time of press, the author and publisher do not assume and hereby disclaim any liability to any party for any loss, damage, or disruption caused by errors or omissions, whether such errors or omissions result from negligence, accident, or any other cause. The information is based on the author's research, knowledge and experience. The facts and theories presented here are subject to the author's interpretation and conclusions and the recommendations presented may not be in alignment or agreement with other interpretations.

I have tried to recreate events, locales, conversations, and experiences from my memories connected to the theories in this book. However, to maintain anonymity in some instances, I have changed the names or have not included names of individuals and places.

Keep in mind that there is no magic trick that will change your life for the better, but through consistency and persistence of the theories taught in this book one can strive in making that lasting change.

Dedication

I wish to dedicate this book to my children, Morgan and Jordan. I am not a perfect mother. In fact, I am not a perfect anything. I am an imperfect expression of the love you give me so freely and unconditionally. I pray you continue to believe that all things are possible and that God is on your side, conspiring to help you win! You will go through things in this life as we all have a path to travel and a divine purpose to fulfill, but I hope you will trust that it all works out for your good in the end. There may be times when you question everything you ever thought you knew or believed to be true and it is then that you will have to look within and listen to that still, small voice that is ever-present and all-knowing. I hope you know that it is my absolute joy being your mother and helping you navigate the waters of this life that are sometimes calm and at other times turbulent. You are each an incredible blend of your father and I with your own special gifts, talents and characteristics that make you different and unique. I thank God for you daily and I pray and cover your minds, your bodies and your spirits. You are my prince and princess and I am honored to be your Sarabi (Lion King). Stay true to yourselves and live unapologetically. Believe in your dreams and always reach for the moon because even if you miss, you will land among the stars!

I love you to infinity & beyond,
Mommy
September 2020

Acknowledgements

First, I want to say thank you God for giving me the vision to write this book and for encouraging me not to sell myself short. I resisted and You persisted. Finally, I surrendered…and Epiphany was born. This book is truly a window into my heart, my soul and my life as it captures the essence of my challenges and struggles and also my growth and evolution.

Secondly, I am grateful to my mother who taught me so many life lessons, even though it did not feel that way at the time. I thank her for giving me life and thereby, giving life to my children and my legacy. I also have to thank my father, whom I never met, but was also instrumental in helping create the person that is me.

Next, I have to thank my amazing husband, Jerome, who has the patience of Job. Literally. LOL. This man is the anchor to my sail and does everything in his power to hold us down while I pursue my purpose and live out my dreams. He supports me, he listens to my ideas, he stands in the gap when I need him to pray and cover me, and he works tirelessly behind the scenes to make sure I always shine. Thank you, babe. Thank you to my incredible children, Morgan and Jordan, for sharing me with world and being patient during all those hours that mommy "was working". You are two of the most loving, kindhearted, and thoughtful people I have ever met. I love you.

I thank my sisters, Tonya and Caryn, who support me without hesitation and are first in line to celebrate me. I thank my family (especially my nieces Tasheka and Latoya and my cousin Tim) for sharing my posts, commenting, promoting, recommending and supporting my efforts. I thank my friends, aka my "Dream Team" (LaDonya, Christy, Audrey, Juanita, Paula, LaTanya, Lisa, Twanja, and Wanda), for always being there with a listening ear and a loving heart and for knowing when to push me and when to embrace me. And I have to thank my sisters in the Breathe Group and the Breathe

Movement for buying into my vision and being there to support this mission. You really are my wing women.

I sincerely thank my mentor, Tobias S. Schreiber, who has always challenged me to explore, examine and express my highest truths. Tobias, you have shared more wisdom with me in the time I have known you than all the books I ever read in graduate school. I am forever grateful for that.

Next, I wish to thank the people who have shown up in my life as opponents and adversaries; you have challenged me to grow and you have taught me some of my greatest life lessons and have been a mirror for me to see inside myself. I can genuinely say that I am grateful for every offense, rejection, betrayal, heartbreak, and everything else it may have taken to get me here. It was worth it and I would gladly do it all over again.

Finally, thank you to my nephew, Shane Burgess, for the amazing photo shoot and back cover photo; Zunaira Saleem (lil sis) for the awesome book cover design, landing page and flyer; Diedra Mills for beating this face for the photo shoot; and Jackie McCullough for slaying my hair as always. Last but definitely not least, I wish to especially thank everyone who purchases and reads this book, for without you, these messages would not reach the four corners of the earth and change thousands of lives in the process. I thank God for your support and your sacrifice.

In Love & Light,
Giovanna

Preface

I have had the privilege and honor of knowing and supervising Giovanna over the past 10 years. She is a courageous and dedicated individual who does not back down from challenges of a blessed and fulfilling life. She is inquisitive, brave and energetic in her pursuit of truth and healing. The great challenge in life is to tolerate the flow of energy through the form and Giovanna accepted and conquered that challenge. She discovered the simple yet powerful tool of Breathe. Breathing is the first and last thing we do on this journey of life. Energy comes in the form of experiences, events and people, and is converted into thoughts feelings, beliefs, fears, hopes and actions. Two great drives of the nervous system are 1. survival and 2. connection /attachment. It is often difficult to connect to the people we are in the world with, without a loss of self. Like most of us, Giovanna gave up her sense of self and her self compassion for the promise that others would fulfill us and complete us. Looking within ourselves, we lose our perception of the world and perceiving the world we lose our sense of self. So, the challenge is to do both simultaneously. The back and forth between these perceptions is difficult and generates many emotions.

Giovanna did the work to become a great therapist in order to help others and she discovered herself by coming face to face with the realization of who she had always been. The Bible states there are two great commandments, the first is to love God with all your, heart, mind, and strength, and the second is to love others as yourself. The world confuses how to love and can often shame us for caring about ourselves. Giovanna regained her sense of self and the wonderment of being. She had an epiphany and a sudden realization of her and our divine nature that is never lost but merely covered up by illusion. All you can teach is understanding, the rest has to come on its own. Once we have a realization or epiphany, it is up to us to live and utilize it each day to reap the benefits. As you read and open yourself to the revelations in Epiphany, you, like I will see a path to self-understanding and love unfold before you and you will discover your own special path.

In her second book, Giovanna offers people a chance to discover who they are and fully embrace the reality of living a blessed and fulfilled life by returning to who you are. The truth of who you are is closer than your next breath. May you accept the opportunity to discover your own epiphany and realize this gift.

"The outer teacher is a manifestation of the inner teacher and the discovery of that is a blessing in itself."

Tobias S. Schreiber, LPC/S

TABLE OF CONTENTS

Introduction

"It probably has a million definitions.
It's the occurrence when the mind, the body, the heart, and
the soul focus together and see an old thing in a new way"
~~Maya Angelou

Epiphany. If I had to choose one word to describe the last three years of my life, this would be it. While I cannot accurately pinpoint the exact moment my journey began, I can say that it was most likely happening in small, miniscule ways all along; however, I did not become fully aware of it or experience the full effect of it until my life started falling apart. At least that was the way it felt.

It was March of 2017 and I had just released my first book, *Why Am I Still Single*, a self-help book on love and relationships that I had been working on for the past nine years. In this book I shared my own story of struggling to find happily ever after, along with insights I gained from family and friends as well as clients in my private psychotherapy practice over the years. The book was a hit! All of a sudden, I was cast into the local and regional spotlight and recognized as a published author. Not only were people purchasing and reading my book, they were eagerly sharing testimonies of the impact my book had made on them; not just in the areas of dating and relationships, but also in the areas of self-love, self-esteem, boundaries, parenting, and their own childhood issues. Married women, single women, divorced women, older women, younger women, women who were in somewhat healthy relationships, and women in abusive relationships were all reading my book and sharing my story. I even had mothers and fathers buying the book for their daughters or other family members. My friends and family were reading it along with some of my fellow therapist colleagues who were also recommending it to their clients. I was in awe. While I always felt the book was going to be great and I hoped and prayed it would change people's lives and heal their relationships, actually seeing and experiencing it was very different. A month after the book was released, I held my first book signing downtown in my hometown of Greenville, SC. Wouldn't you know it, it rained. And not just a sprinkle or a light drizzle, but an incessant downpour that lasted most of the day. I worried whether, given the circumstance, anyone would actually show up (I wasn't entirely sure that I would have come had it been someone else's event), but when I walked out of the room where I was having my makeup done, the theatre was almost filled to capacity. "Wow", I thought, as I realized that all of these people had braved the storm and come out to see and celebrate me. As I stood there in back of the theatre, listening to one person after the other share insights and testimonies about my book, I felt a mixture of both excitement and humility at the same time.

After my initial book signing, I went on to host other book promotional events in the area and my husband hired a public relations expert out of Indiana to help me gain exposure outside of Upstate SC. All of a sudden, I was being featured in national print and online publications such as the HuffPost, Sheen Magazine and Black Enterprise. I also was being asked to do podcast and radio interviews across the country. People were inviting me to speak to churches, book clubs, women's ministries, colleges and conferences, and people from all over began following me on Facebook and direct messaging me. I was having the time of my life doing what I loved, promoting my book and speaking on the topic of healthy relationships to anyone who would listen. Little did I know that just a few months later, everything would change. While many people were genuinely happy for me and supporting my rise to success, not everyone was celebrating. That meant nothing to me as I had already decided that as long as I had the support of my inner circle...my husband, my family and my friends, then I was okay with other people "out there" not supporting and celebrating me. In some ways, I was even prepared for it. What I was not prepared for however, was when things began to shift inside my inner circle and relationships with longtime friends ended or became significantly strained and distant. I felt confused, hurt, angry and betrayed, and what made it worse was I had no idea how to fix it. Other people attempted to remind me that people are in our lives for a reason, a season or a lifetime and when they have served their purpose or their season has ended, life will either remove them or they will remove themselves. Even though I was familiar with this saying and I believed it to be true, that did little to ease the emotional pain I was experiencing on the inside. I asked myself why and when no answers appeared, I began to blame myself and question everything and everyone around me.

It was during that questioning and seeking God that my season of discovery, revelation, insight, awareness and transformation began as I started to receive epiphany after epiphany, feeling my soul awaken for the first time in my life. I had read many popular books about transformation, spiritual enlightenment and self-awareness including *The Celestine Prophecy* by James Redfield and everything by Iyanla Vanzant, before she was a household name. I became a fan of Oprah Winfrey, Deepak Chopra, Dr. Wayne Dyer, Louise Hay, Lisa Nichols, Mark Victor Hansen, Les Brown and Tony Robbins, to name a few. When I reflect on it now, I was always seeking deeper knowledge, meaning, wisdom and understanding. Perhaps it comes from my love of reading, or maybe it is part of the fabric that makes me who I am; either way, this period of loneliness, isolation, desolation, and transition became the catalyst for my inner healing, transformation and ultimately my freedom.

As I spent quiet time alone with God and myself, I started to receive what I call "downloads" of incredible eye-opening wisdom, insight, and revelation that enabled me to experience one aha moment after the other. An epiphany is defined as a moment of sudden revelation, insight or manifestation that completely changes your perspective and the ways in which you view yourself and the world around you. In her book by the same title, author and actress Elise Ballard, shares a collective definition of epiphany that came as the result of several people she interviewed for her book, including Maya Angelou. Her definition and description of an epiphany is: "A dawning: a realization: an opening; a portal to the Divine: growing up: a magic moment that impacts you and changes you forever and you can remember it as vividly as you experienced it; a moment that changes the lens through which you view your life: our soul scratching around our heads and giving us a signal to guide our lives with: a moment of descending light, open knowledge, and choice: a drastic shift in energy and change of perspective that happens in the form of a moment of clarity and understanding: something that gives you the strength to take a different direction or move forward, and opens up everything: a sense of wonderment: a clarifying direction: and, that moment where you know you and your life are never going to be the same". As so eloquently defined in that definition, I can honestly state that my level of insight and understanding went deeper than it had ever gone before, and my mind expanded in ways I had never experienced. I truly felt my soul open itself up to endless possibilities and I began seeing myself and everything around me in a whole different light. I knew I was never going to be the same.

One of my favorite quotes is "When the student is ready, the teacher appears." During that time, I would often joke that it felt as if God, The Holy Spirit, The Divine Feminine, and Jesus all became my teachers and coaches and life became my classroom. I would say to my husband that I could not put a price tag on the "education" I was receiving.

It was also during that time of my life, which felt like being in a dark tunnel, that I discovered something that I now live by and frequently share with clients, "The way out is through". Even though I wanted nothing more than for this phase of my life to end and to come out of that dark space I was in, the reality is that sometimes our greatest opportunities for healing and restoration are found in the midst of our most painful experiences. Turkish philosopher, Rumi stated that "The cure for pain is in the pain" and the truth is that most of us, myself included, would rather avoid, deny, and ignore our pain than face up to our fears, insecurities and uncertainties. We just want a way out...out of the loneliness, out of the discomfort, the pain, the fear, the anxiety, the anger and the depression, without fully understanding that the way out is actually through the situation and not around it. Many times, we may even seek out unhealthy ways to numb and alleviate our pain altogether such as overeating, overspending, overcommitting ourselves, overextending, or self-medicating through the use of sex, drugs and alcohol. Unfortunately, our painful experiences and emotions will not just go away, fade over time or be forgotten simply because we have chosen to bury and ignore them. We cannot go around or go over, sometimes we have to go through and the important thing is not *that* we go through, but *how* we go through.

I was in session with a client one day explaining this same concept when all of a sudden, I saw an image of a mountain with a tunnel going through it and in that moment, I realized that the dark tunnel we sometimes feel we are in is actually how we get through to the other side. Even though it may be scary, unfamiliar, and seemingly unending, eventually we see light at the end of the tunnel and it will lead us to the other side if we just hang in there and stay the course.

It was during the session with this client that I also recognized that my own dark tunnel was my way through and I would not be able to go over or around it. I too had to go through. So often, we pray and ask for change and growth, until life begins to offer us opportunities disguised as challenges to help bring about our transformation. As much as I hurt during that time and as much as I hated to admit it, I knew I could no longer avoid my own lessons in living. My requests to grow, heal, change, transform and live my best life had led me into my own dark tunnel and I was going to have to go through it to reach the other side.

Looking back, I can remember how people were praising and congratulating me for the accomplishments and successes they were witnessing on the outside, while I was saying silently to myself, "If you only knew what is happening on the inside". One of the seven principles of Hermes Trismegistus is "As Within, So Without", which essentially means that whatever is happening on the inside of us, will eventually show up on the outside. So, when you and I set out to make any significant changes in our lives, the first place we must begin is within.

My former pastor once preached a sermon in which he told us that instead of trying to fix all the issues of our hearts (which can be many), we should focus on fixing our hearts. What I did not know or understand at the time, is that I would be required to "fix my heart" or more accurately, I would be required to heal my heart. Unfortunately, we have been taught to focus on the outer world, the issues of our hearts rather than our hearts, which is why we are more depressed, unhappy and unfulfilled than ever, even though we have access to everything we could possibly think and imagine.

For years, I have been studying self-help and self-improvement concepts that have taught me that what we think, believe, feel, and speak shapes our behavior and our perceptions and these perceptions become our reality. This is why we must begin within and equally the reason why our happiness is an inside job, our success is an inside job, good health is an inside job, wealth and abundance is an inside job and healing is an inside job.

Epiphany is the story of my own journey of discovery, enlightenment, awakening, healing, growth and transformation, as I learned the importance of living life from the inside out. Epiphany is a in depth look at the ups and downs, failures and successes, and gains and losses I have experienced during the past few years. I have shed many tears in this season and have had to travel to some of the deepest darkest places within myself, coming face to face with truths about me and the world around me that I would have preferred to keep hidden from everyone, including God. I have chosen to write this story and share my journey with you along with all of the lessons, blessings, wisdom, insight, knowledge and understanding I have gained and discovered; however, this in no way signifies that I have arrived or that I have it all figured out. Life is a journey, not a destination, and when all is said and done, that is what truly matters. The word journey itself is defined as a passage from one place to another, and I want each person reading this book to not only become familiar with my journey, but to also embark upon your own journey of discovery, awareness, awakening and enlightenment as you develop a deeper understanding and awareness of who you authentically are and what really motivates you from within.

As you read each chapter and reflect on the thought provoking questions at the end, I hope you will experience your own epiphanies, aha moments and revelations. There is also space provided for you to capture any immediate downloads and insights. If you need more room to fully work through the assignments, I encourage you to purchase the Epiphany Discovery Journal (being released at a later date) where you will have the opportunity to fully process and expand your level of understanding. It is my prayer that at the end of this book, you will have discovered and fallen madly in love with the greatest person you will ever meet: You.

Here we go…

Chapter 1

Who Are You?

"Knowing yourself is the beginning of all wisdom"
~~Aristotle

One of the most profound discoveries I made during my season of epiphany is how important and essential it is for us to know who we are. Not just our physically defining characteristics such as height, weight and eye color or even our race, ethnicity and cultural features, but we are each meant to rediscover who we really are and reconnect with the parts of us that may be long hidden and forgotten. I had my first opportunity to reflect on the question, "Who Am I", in March 2018 during a four-day personal development training in NYC. Throughout the weekend, our instructor continually posed this question to us until eventually I began to realize that he wasn't simply asking us for information that could be found on our social media profiles or in our professional biographies; he was asking us a question that was designed to make us look within for the answers. Who am I? I had signed up to attend this training not knowing what to expect, and being that I was alone and the only person in the room from SC, I immediately began to rely on the things that caused me to feel a sense of identity and accomplishment within myself. Who am I? Before this experience, I thought I knew exactly who I was and how to answer that question. "I am an African-American woman in my late forties who was born and raised in a small town in Upstate SC to a single mother. I have two sisters, four brothers (two of whom are now deceased), and a huge extended family. Professionally, I am a licensed psychotherapist in private practice, a life coach, author, speaker and a former radio talk show host. Oh, you want to know more? I am a happily married mother of two; a boy and a girl, a homeowner and I drive a nearly new SUV. I also pride myself on being genuine and authentic, and part of my platform is in empowering women to discover their own truths and become the greatest versions of themselves. There. That is who I am." What I did not fully understand at the time, is that once all of my titles and externally defining characteristics were removed, I would be left feeling extremely vulnerable, exposed and "busted". More so, I would discover before the end of that weekend just how truly irrelevant and unimportant those things really were and I would be forced to face and confront the whole truth of who I really was: the good, the bad and the ugly.

Truth be told, I have struggled most of my life with knowing who I am. Of course, I knew my name, date of birth, race and other physical attributes just as I was equally aware of basic things such as my favorite foods, colors, music and clothing style. I knew that my personality was outgoing, extroverted and generally optimistic. I knew what sparked my anger, my passion and also what caused me to feel warm and fuzzy, but I did not fully know who I was at my core. I had been wearing a mask for so long and acting out of a false identity that when I really began my self-examination, I discovered parts of myself that felt completely foreign and unknown to me. In my first book, I shared how being raised without my father had left me with an internal need for validation, affirmation, approval, and acceptance. For years I struggled with my identity and knowing who I was which lead to a constant search outside of myself. When I could not find what I was seeking in my relationships, I tried to identify myself through my achievements. Throughout my entire life, I had never been advised or encouraged to look inside myself or to provide myself with the internal things I needed. Like many of us, I grew up believing that self-reliance, self-affirmation, self-acceptance, self-approval, self-love, and self-validation was "self-ish". Thank God I now know that this is not true and the reality of it is that we are born with an inner sense of who and what we are and also what we came here to do. Unfortunately, due to certain painful experiences in life such as abuse, rejection, abandonment, and neglect, we start forgetting this inner truth and begin to identify and define ourselves by what has happened to us and what our experiences and other people have taught us. What I have now discovered is that who we really are is so much bigger and more powerful than many of us know or understand. Who we are goes beyond our titles, positions, or possessions and I, like everyone else, am already whole, complete and lacking nothing? Anything that contradicts this is merely an illusion and a distortion in our perception. Sometimes it can be upsetting when we first realize this as we reflect on all the time we have wasted trying to prove ourselves and pursue some false sense of perfection that we will never be able to reach and attain.

Whenever I have clients come to me saying they feel lost and don't know who they are, I suggest to them that perhaps instead of being lost, they have simply hidden or disconnected from their true selves. I love how Emily McDowell puts it, "Finding yourself is not really how it works. You aren't a ten-dollar bill in last winter's coat pocket. You are not lost. Your true self is right there, buried under cultural conditioning, other people's opinions, and inaccurate conclusions you drew as a kid that became your beliefs about who you are. Finding yourself is actually returning to yourself. An unlearning, an excavation, a remembering who you were before the world got its hands on you." I now believe that each of us comes to the planet with an exact blueprint of who we are and what we were designed to do. Whenever I have clients who had horrible childhood experiences as the result of parents who were abusive, neglectful, unavailable, or otherwise just not great people, I suggest to them that if their mother and/or father did nothing else right, they made them and if their only job was to get them into the earth to fulfill their divine mission and purpose, then they had done their part. I understand some of us have had very painful experiences that have caused us to question ourselves and doubt our very existence, but I am here to inform you that you are an essential element in the grand design of the universe and while you may want to uncover what appears to be hidden and unknown, or heal any areas in need of healing, you still get to love and accept yourself unconditionally and embrace the truth that you are already whole, perfect and complete.

Personal Reflection:

1) Who are you at the core of your being? Who were you around age five? When did things start to shift for you?

2) What if what you have been seeking is already on the inside of you waiting for you to uncover, discover and recover it??

3) How might things shift for you if you accept that you are already whole and complete?

Chapter 2

There Is Only Love

"How You Love Yourself Is How You Teach Others to Love You"
~~Rupi Kaur

Although I am writing this chapter last, it is perhaps one of, if not *the* most important messages in this entire book. Love. Not just the word we use to describe feelings of romance or affection, but love in all of its simplicity, perfection and completeness. What is love? Love is one of those words that when mentioned brings up all sorts of images, ideas, memories, thoughts and feelings of past or current experiences. The Greeks have several names to define the different types of love. The first kind of love is Eros or romantic love, and it represents feelings of attraction, passion and desire. While Eros can be beautiful and exciting, it can also lead to unhealthy behaviors such as codependency, abuse, impulsivity, obsession, jealousy, possession, and even murder as the strong, intense feelings produced by Eros love can be as addictive as drugs.

The second type of love is Philia, brotherly love, and it refers to the deep love and affection between friends, without sexual attraction. The third type is Storge and similar to Philia, Storge is the love between family members. Although it is a powerful form of love, Storge can also be a reason people do not progress in life. I know many people who have failed to fully pursue their dreams either because they lacked the support and encouragement of their family members or they feared their criticism, rejection or abandonment. The fourth kind of love is Agape, often described as an unconditional, selfless love that is extended to everyone including family members and complete strangers. Agape is often referred to in Christianity as the love of God for man and the love of man for God. Agape is also seen as the love of a parent for a child. The fifth type of love, Philautia, self-love, is considered to be essential for any relationship we have because we cannot fully love others if we do not love ourselves first.

Many of us have now become aware of the importance of loving ourselves in addition to loving God and others. I see countless clients who are struggling with low self-esteem, poor self-image, low self-worth, depression, anxiety and suicidal ideation because they were never taught the importance of loving themselves. In many cases, people have been taught that self-love is self-centered, self-absorbed and selfish which has caused them to carry heavy feelings of guilt and instead focus all of their efforts on loving others while negating the crucial necessity of also loving themselves. As within, so without - which means that I must love me first, before I can even know how to love someone else. Otherwise, I will always seek others to fill my love tank and possibly end up feeling empty, depleted and resentful if and when they do not or cannot reciprocate. Self-love is not selfish or self-centered. In fact, the opposite is true. The absence of self-love is what breeds self-centeredness and self-absorption because of the person's internal need to overcompensate for what is perceived to be lacking or missing. Loving ourselves is about loving and accepting our internal and external flaws, character defects, insecurities and shortcomings without judgment or criticism, extending to ourselves the grace, forgiveness, compassion and understanding that we so often and so freely give to others. I now believe that self-love and self-acceptance are two of the most powerful gifts we can ever give to ourselves.

In my first book, I shared that we attract what we are and not what we want, so rather than offer women tips on how to get the man they wanted, I encouraged them to learn the importance of loving themselves first if they wanted to attract a partner who would love them in return. Every relationship we have flows from the one we have with ourselves. From the relationships we had or have with our parents, our siblings, friends, neighbors, colleagues, and even our romantic partners. All of these relationships are wonderfully revealing indicators of the internal relationship we have with ourselves and the way we feel about ourselves. I often state that people do not treat us the way we treat them, people treat us the way we treat ourselves. If we are negative, judgmental, and overly self-critical of ourselves, then we will often find that many people in our lives view and treat us in a much similar way. The partner or supervisor that always seems to criticize us, find fault in what we do or that we never seem to please is simply the mirror that is revealing to us the way we view and feel about ourselves. You and I are powerful magnets that are continually attracting the people and the circumstances we encounter in our lives even if we are unaware of it. If we are constantly attracting people who lie to us, betray or mistreat us, then it is our responsibility to explore and identify why this pattern keeps showing up. I have discovered that life is for us and because of this, life will send us the lessons and the experiences that are necessary to propel us into becoming everything we are meant to be. For example, the mate who betrays you may have shown up to reveal that you were settling for less than what you deserved.

We cannot merely say we love ourselves without the corresponding actions to show and prove it. I have met so many people who professed to love themselves until I examined their lives and saw everything *except* a love for self, from people in abusive relationships and living in situations where they are unfulfilled and dissatisfied, settling in jobs they hate or remaining in friendships they have long outgrown. Love is an action. It is not enough to just say I love me; I have to also act in ways that are loving. When working with clients in this area, I often ask them to picture a person they love unconditionally, be it a parent, child, friend, or partner. Time and again, I witness their faces lighting up and their voices becoming softer as they describe the love they feel for this person. Then I ask them to replace the image of this person with themselves. Oftentimes there is an immediate shift in their facial expressions as they wrestle with this only to eventually admit that they cannot imagine extending this type of love to themselves. This is where the work for all of us begins. We have to love ourselves first. We have to be loyal to ourselves first. We have to be dedicated, honest, faithful, and committed to ourselves first.

I must admit, this has not been easy for me, especially as someone who never knew or understood the value of loving myself and who continually sought external love and acceptance from others. I had to learn to fall in love with me and to do that, I had to get to know me and be honest with myself about who I have been, who I am and who I am meant to be. I had to learn to love "me the person" beyond my accomplishments, titles, appearance, relationships, economic status, or even my purpose. I literally had to strip away anything that I "took on" and get to the core of my very existence and start there. I had to face up to and own my own shit, doing it in such a way as not to diminish it or whitewash it, but to accept it and make peace with it. As I grow and evolve, I am discovering that my love for myself continues to deepen, widen and expand and I understand that this process of self-love will be a life-long experience of awakening, awareness, and acceptance.

I invite you to spend some time thinking about what it means to fall in love with yourself, first. Understand that this is not some shallow, narcissistic, conceited type of love or admiration, but a deeply transformational "process" of loving yourself without fear, judgment, criticism, doubt, condemnation, or comparison to anyone and everyone else. It means simply loving you for the very fact that you exist. It is not about your accomplishments and awards, your physical appearance, your financial status, material possessions, social network followers, relationship status or even your lifestyle. It is about loving you because you *are* you. Loving you with all of your character flaws, insecurities, past experiences, and personality traits, and really accepting yourself for the person you are right now instead of waiting to love you when you become the person you desire to be or believe you should be. Give yourself permission to love yourself NOW. There is no need to wait or fix yourself or become anything other than what you are. You deserve the best of you right now and I encourage you not to go one more day without learning to fill your own love tank and meeting your own emotional needs within.

The Force of Love

Even though the Greeks had different words to describe different types of love, when you get right down to it, there is only love. And love is not simply a feeling or emotion, love is a universal force of energy. Nobel Peace prize winning physicist, Albert Einstein, is reported to have written a letter to his daughter Liesel shortly before his death that said, "There is an extremely powerful force that includes and governs all others, and is even behind any phenomenon operating in the universe. This force explains everything and gives meaning to life, and each individual carries within them a small but powerful generator of love whose energy is waiting to be released. When we give and receive this universal energy, we will have affirmed that love conquers all, and is able to transcend everything and anything, because love is the quintessence of life". In the book, *The Power,* Rhonda Byrne - who also wrote *The Secret* - speaks about love as a force that has the power to heal our bodies, transform our relationships, attract to us our desires and help us bring about almost any condition we wish to experience. Rhonda urges us to harness the power of love to overcome most of our physical, emotional, mental and spiritual hardships so that we can live our best lives imaginable. When I first read *The Power* almost two years ago, I can remember having to take breaks between chapters just to allow myself time to absorb the enormity of wisdom I was being taught. Not only was this book answering many of my life questions, it was doing so in a way that was mind-blowing and life changing. In the two years since my initial introduction to *The Power*, I have listened to it audibly and read and re-read it numerous times because it continues to speak to me in new and exciting ways as my understanding of its concepts and ideologies deepens. To date, it is one of the absolute best books I have ever read and I have read thousands of books during my lifetime. Perhaps it is because the insights contained within the book are things that I have known inwardly but dared not pretend I knew because it went against everything I had been taught to believe. Sure, I grew up hearing that God is love and that I was to love my neighbor as myself. Yes, I loved my family, my friends, my husband, my children and I eventually figured out how to love myself, but the idea of love as a life changing force was an extreme shift in consciousness that stretched me beyond any of my past or current understanding and ignited explosions of awareness, awakening and enlightenment for the first time in my life. God is love and God as love is such a deeper, more expansive way of thinking, feeling, perceiving and being than anything I have ever experienced and I realize as cliché or hokey as it sounds, *love*, really is all we need. Since I committed myself to growing in love, walking in love and living in love, I can see how certain things that used to be okay are no longer okay for me. I am now accountable for what I know and believe and I realize that things such as gossip, criticism, judgment, fault finding or complaining are no longer just harmless forms of self-expression. Now that I know the price we pay for holding onto things such as grudges, offenses and unforgiveness, I have to be willing to release people from any mental, emotional or relational indebtedness. I can no longer justify or rationalize my right to stay angry or upset at someone for something, as I now know that every cell in my body receives messages from me based on my thoughts and feelings and those messages can be either positive and life-giving or negative and life-draining, and because my positive and negative vibrations are being broadcast into the physical world around me, I am literally creating my reality and my experiences.

A few years ago, I began studying the connection between emotions and our physical bodies, and while it has been a slow process to admit and accept this wholeheartedly, I am now convinced that there is truth to it. Books such as *The Body Keeps the Score* by Bessel Van Der Kolk, MD; The *Emotion Code* by Dr. Bradley Nelson; *You Can Heal Your Life* by Louise Hay; or *Feelings Buried Alive Never Die* by Karol K. Truman are just a few of the resources that expound on this direct correlation between our thoughts, emotions, feelings, and our physical bodies. Karol K. Truman's book even includes a glossary that lists common physical ailments and their corresponding unresolved emotional issues. In working with clients, I have begun to see firsthand evidence of this connection in the clients I work with and also in my own life. When we hold onto negative toxic emotions, feelings and memories, it can cause blockages in our energy system that can prevent us from experiencing true joy, happiness, and peace. These energetic blocks can also cause us to have high levels of stress that may develop into mental and emotional conditions such as depression and anxiety. Over time, it is believed that our emotional blockages manifest into physical blockages that become issues such as indigestion, gas, bloating and constipation. There are theories holding that every physical ailment, condition or disease has within it an unresolved emotional component. Bruce Tainio, developer of the Tainio Technology, found that the human body resonates at a frequency of 62 MHz. When the body's frequency drops below 58 MHz, bacteria, viruses and disease can begin. We are now beginning to understand everything in the universe vibrates and has its own unique frequency, from plants and animals to music and food. It is also believed that feelings and emotions have frequencies and these frequencies can and do affect how we feel. Feelings such as joy, hope, passion, excitement, and gratitude have a high frequency and therefore cause us to feel good. Likewise, feelings such as guilt, anger, sadness, shame, despair, jealousy, hatred, and rage have low frequencies and cause us to feel bad. At the end of the day, it is all about energy, frequency and vibration and *love* is one of the highest frequencies that exists alongside joy, peace and enlightenment. Even the Bible speaks of love as being greater than faith and hope, so when we truly begin to walk in love, we understand that what we feel, think, say and do not only affects us or those close to us, but it affects everything and everyone in the world around us. Ultimately, there is no her, him, they or them, for what I do to someone else is what I also do to myself. We reap what we sow. When we sow hatred, anger, criticism, judgment or unforgiveness, we live with the fruits of these emotional vices and it is said that our negativity doesn't just return to us, it returns to us multiplied. We may not always make the connection between our marriage ending with things we have said or done to someone else. We may not connect our financial struggles with a grudge we are still holding against someone. We may not see the sickness in our bodies as being the result of racism, sexism, injustice and intolerance. I have come to realize that I cannot just speak in love, I have to live in love because this is the absolute best way for me to serve God, myself and the planet. The book, *The Power*, gives countless examples of how the force of love has been used to restore broken relationships, heal sickness and disease, increase wealth and prosperity, manifest dreams and desires, eliminate debt, and many other amazing things. Honestly, when you think about it, we cannot afford NOT to love; not if we want to have and live an amazing, abundant life. Maybe there's a good reason that Jesus only left us with two commandments which were to love God and love our neighbors as ourselves.

I am steadily growing in love for myself, others and the world around me, and daily, I give thanks for my family, my marriage, my children, my friends, my health and everything else. I even give thanks to and for my body which allows me to experience the world through my five senses. Because of my body, I can feel a hug from my children or a kiss from my husband. Without it, I could not witness a gorgeous sunset or watch waves cresting in the ocean. I could not hear the sounds of beautiful music or my children playing. As I am learning to live from a state of love and gratitude, I am noticing that my entire perspective is shifting and expanding. During my daily walks, I frequently find myself overjoyed by simple things such as a caterpillar crawling on the ground, birds singing in the trees, or a gentle breeze blowing across my face. I am filled with joy and excitement even on otherwise ordinary days, and I am kinder, more compassionate and understanding towards myself and others.

My love journey is far from over, perfect or complete and sometimes I still have to make a conscious decision to choose love, especially during a time when there is so much unrest and injustice in the world. Some days, it feels like it would be so much easier to choose judgment, criticism, hatred, pride, or revenge. It would be easy to become angry and retaliate against those who cannot and will not love people who look like me; but what purpose does that serve? Hate doesn't change things, love does; and because I understand that I can still love someone and abhor their actions, choosing love is really my only choice. When I respond in kind to my enemies, it causes me to sink to the same level and vibration they are on, which ultimately brings harm to me, not them. Let me be clear though, because I do not want to portray choosing love as a passive thing nor do I mean for people to condone bad behavior or allow others to walk all over them. In fact, it is quite the opposite. Choosing love means still holding people accountable for their actions. But hating someone because they hate you requires you to give away your power and define yourself by someone else's actions. That is simply too high a price to pay.

As you embark on your own journey of love for yourself and for others, I advise you to choose wisely and do not allow yourself to be weakened by heavy emotions such as judgment, hatred, racism, criticism, sexism, or fear even when that seems to be the easy or logical choice. Love *has* power and love *is* power and we can use the power of love to transform our lives and the world in which we live.

Personal Reflection:

1) Are you still waiting for permission from someone in order to love yourself? (A parent, sibling, partner, ex-partner, teacher, friend, etc.)

2) Are you waiting until you are perfect to love yourself?

3) What can you do today to begin the process of falling in love with you or loving others more openly and unconditionally?

4) What areas of your life could be improved by the force of love?

Chapter 3

Self-Acceptance & Validation

"If You Live for People's Acceptance,
You Will Die from Their Rejection."
~~Lecrae

In addition to learning the importance of loving ourselves and others, I have also begun to recognize the need and the freedom that comes from accepting and validating ourselves. Self-acceptance is defined as satisfaction or happiness with oneself as well as having self-understanding and awareness of one's individual strengths and weaknesses. Psychologists purport that it is a necessary element of good mental and emotional health, as well as all-round well-being. I believe self-acceptance is highly essential to our healing, our growth and our level of happiness and contentment in life. Since every relationship we have flows from the one we have with ourselves, we have to learn to accept ourselves and all of our "stuff" or it is going to be nearly impossible for someone else to accept us as we are, for who we are. Not only have I had to work through this in my own life, I have seen it show up countless times in my work with clients. Men and women who have never realized the importance of accepting themselves because they have come to me expecting me to fix them by helping them change some behavior, thought, or feeling. While I certainly recognize that all of us may have areas in need of healing, I always set the foundation for the healing process by beginning with the need for self-acceptance. This is often difficult at first because most of us believe that we cannot be acceptable to others or ourselves until we have fixed every flaw, healed every broken place, eliminated all negative thoughts and "bad" feelings, and are damn near perfect. As a result, we go through life judging, condemning, comparing, criticizing, neglecting, rejecting, denying, mistreating and even abusing ourselves while simultaneously seeking the external acceptance, approval and validation of others. Sadly, many of us have never known or understood the necessity, the beauty and the freedom that is inherent in learning to accept ourselves instead of spending our whole lives seeking the acceptance of everyone else and ignoring the importance of beginning within.

Learning to accept ourselves is not about pretending and ignoring the habits, attitudes, thoughts or behaviors we may desire to change or even need to change. It is also not an excuse to justify bad behavior nor is it a resignation that things cannot or will not change. It is not about complacency, settling, condoning or even liking everything about ourselves. Self-acceptance is about fully receiving ourselves as we are right now with all of our deficiencies, flaws, shortcomings, failures, past experiences, fears and insecurities without judgment, blame, condemnation, criticism, rejection or comparison to others. Self-acceptance is based on understanding who we are, our strengths and weaknesses and allowing ourselves permission to be less than perfect. In positive psychology, self-acceptance is seen as the basis for any change to occur, because when we resist parts of ourselves or things about ourselves, we may actually prevent those things from changing. The Law of Attraction says that what we resist, persists, so when we refuse to accept a part of ourselves, we are actually causing the very thing we want to change to remain. This may lead us to believe we are powerless to change when the reality is that accepting them with love and compassion is what opens the door for change to occur. It is leaning into it, rather than pushing it away, allowing us to operate from the reality that we are already complete rather than from the illusion that we are broken or lacking.

In my own life, I have had to learn to accept myself and overcome the need to fix myself and strive for perfection. Accepting myself does not mean I do not desire growth or self-improvement, I just no longer have an internal belief that I am inadequate, incomplete, inferior or defective and in constant need of fixing. I once read a quote that said "When I accept myself, I am freed from the burden of needing you to accept me". Self -acceptance, like most things, is an inside job. We cannot get from others what we are not willing to give to ourselves. When we accept ourselves, it is our way of saying to the universe that we are acceptable and we will then attract the people, events and circumstances that align with our belief. So rather than seeking the acceptance of others, we must begin within. I now believe that self-acceptance and self-love are absolutely critical if we are to truly become whole, happy, and healthy.

Just as important as it is to learn the value of self-love and self-acceptance, it is equally important to know what it means to validate ourselves. According to Wikipedia, the word validation comes from the root word valid and is defined as proving the validity or accuracy of something and declaring it acceptable. It also means recognizing that a person's opinions, feelings and ideas are valid and worthwhile. As children, it is normal for us to seek validation from our parents, caregivers and other people of influence such as teachers or coaches. We show up, perform, speak and behave in ways designed to gain the acceptance, approval, affirmation and validation of those around us because receiving validation from others helps us to feel acceptable, necessary, valued, and worthy. When we fail to receive the validation we naturally seek in childhood and our feelings, opinions and ideas are ignored, rejected, or criticized, we often begin to internalize those things and draw the conclusion that *we* are actually unacceptable, unworthy, unnecessary, and insignificant.

In my private practice, I work with adult men and women who are still struggling with the need for validation and affirmation because this need was not met in childhood. Whether it was a parent who was physically or emotionally absent or one who was abusive and neglectful, children who do not have these basic needs met will grow into adults who are still seeking external validation outside of themselves. They will still look to someone else to make them feel worthwhile, important, wanted and valued and they will seek this out in their romantic relationships, friendships, and work relationships. These adults will also find themselves constantly trying to prove their worth and receive validation by accomplishing goals, acquiring material possessions and maintaining a certain outward appearance. Unfortunately, many of us have not yet learned that once we reach adulthood, it becomes our responsibility to validate and affirm ourselves. In fact, when we become adults, we become able to meet our own emotional needs and fill our own love tanks. External validation is when our sense of who we are and how good we are comes from other people, our achievements and our possessions.

Because I grew up without my father, I was constantly seeking external validation through other people, friendships, relationships, and even family members. The reality is that I had to look within me for what I was seeking from them and I had to validate me without any outside influence. Sure, other people in my life have affirmed me and validated me, but none of that mattered until I did it for myself first. I had to learn the hard way to validate myself from inside, rather than seeking external validation through my work, relationships, or accomplishments.

A few years back, my mentor, Tobias Schrieber, taught me that life is meant to be lived from inside out, not from the outside in and that I would never fill an internal need from an external source. Even when it appeared to work, the effects would only be temporary and eventually I would find myself again seeking validation from someone or something. I learned that when I reject and neglect my own ideas, opinions or feelings because I need someone else's consent, agreement or confirmation, then I am not loving myself, valuing myself or even being a good friend to myself. I had to learn to validate my own sense of self-worth and tell myself who I am and that I am good, despite what my experiences or others may have said contrarily.

I have now discovered that the reason so many people continue to struggle with a need for validation is because they are still looking outside of themselves for what will only be found within. I am convinced that everything we need to become who and what we are meant to be, is already inside of us and the key is for us to look within to discover it. I once heard Dr. Myles Munroe say that God has hidden our greatest gifts and potential in the one place He knew we would not overlook it...inside of us. When you think about it, what else makes sense? Why would it be anywhere else when there is a chance we could bypass it?

We must be willing to look inside of ourselves and develop a sense of internal validation. Internal validation is the understanding and acceptance that we have value, worth and purpose regardless of anyone or anything else and that we really do not need external confirmation, approval or agreement. Sure, we may value the opinions of others and it may feel great to have their praise, support and encouragement, but when we depend on that as our only source or the main source of our worth and value, things can become a bit hairy because we are living our lives according to outside influences rather than from our own internal knowingness and intuitiveness. Take it from me, few people will ever know you as well as you know you so I encourage you be willing to initiate the process of self-discovery, learning to like, love, accept and validate yourself to ensure that your internal voice becomes your most trusted and valued source.

Personal Reflection:

1) What would it look and feel like to completely accept yourself with all of your flaws, shortcomings, insecurities, etc.?

2) How would you show up differently? How would your life be different?

3) In what ways have you sought out validation from other people?

4) Do you only feel valued when others confirm and agree with you?

5) What would self-validation from inside of you look and feel like?

Chapter 4

Nothing to Prove

"An Amazing Thing Happens When You
Stop Seeking Approval and Validation: You Find It"
~~Mandy Hale

Christian author and televangelist, Joyce Meyer, wrote a book called *Approval Seeking*. I remember being intrigued by the title when I saw it the first time and wondering what it meant. As I began to examine my own life, I asked myself if I had been seeking the approval of others. The answer was a loud and resounding "Yes". Even as I write this chapter, I am still working to overcome my need for approval from people, even though I know that approval is another one of those things that is an inside job and becomes our responsibility to fulfill once we reach adulthood. Developmentally, it is natural for children to desire and seek the approval of others outside of themselves. It is part of how we develop as human beings. As children we draw pictures, sing songs and perform well in sports or academics, all so we can gain the approval of the people around us. If we receive their approval in a loving, consistent manner, then we develop a healthy sense of internal self-worth and validation from an early age. If we are not approved of and instead are criticized, judged, or ignored, then we develop an internal belief that we are lacking, not good enough, not worthy and or that we are inherently flawed or defective in some way. This may cause us to go through life trying to reconcile these internal feelings and gain approval from others thinking that if others approve of us, their approval will be evidence of our worth. This does not mean that we cannot ask for advice or input from others, but it does mean that if their advice or opinions differ greatly or slightly from our own, we do not immediately second guess, doubt, or invalidate our own thoughts, opinions and ideas. Without learning to approve of ourselves, we may go through life constantly needing other people to agree, consent, confirm, and cosign with us in order to ensure that we have value. In some ways, it is as if we are silently asking permission for us to be who we are and basing our self-concept on the responses and reactions we receive. At least, that was my story.

I was the sixth child of seven, born months after the death of my father who never even knew my mother was expecting. As a result, I believe I came into the world seeking approval from my mother, my family and the father I would never know or meet. I can remember feeling petrified at age five when it was time for me to start school. I was not ready to leave the comfort of my home and enter a world of the unknown. In fact, I was still trying to figure out where I fit in my own family, much less trying to fit in the outside world. Academically, I did well in school and I made some close friends and by the time I was in middle school, I was beginning to feel a sense of belonging. It was then that my oldest sister put a chemical relaxer in my hair that eventually caused all of my hair to fall out over the next few months. I can recall not wanting to go to school for fear of being teased and laughed at by my peers. Having been considered one of the "pretty girls" in school, I felt ugly and literally wanted to disappear until my hair grew back. Finally, my hair did grow back as I entered high school, but because of my need for approval and validation, this was also when my people pleasing behavior began. Throughout my life, the messages I had received from the outside world were that I was flawed, unattractive, abandoned by my own father, overlooked in my own family, and unworthy. I constantly compared myself to my friends, classmates, and family members and I always felt like I failed to measure up or be good enough. In turn, this made me try even harder to gain approval and acceptance. Despite the close friends I had and my popularity in school, I still felt like I was always on the outside looking in. Of course, being sexually molested did nothing to help my self-esteem, self-confidence, or self-image and only served to prompt even more feelings of shame, self-blame and self-rejection. Not only did I seek approval from my mother and my family, I also sought it from other adults. My tenth grade English teacher became the first person in my life who I felt saw me, accepted me and approved of me, when she discovered and encouraged my love of writing. This teacher helped me to find my voice and I began writing every chance I got, from plays to short stories and poetry. I even had a poem published in a national literary magazine. Fast forward to high school when I met my first real boyfriend who became the second person in my life to see me, accept me and approve of me. I was head over heels in love with him and I just knew he would become my husband. We dated for almost four years until the day I accidentally discovered that he was writing love letters to my younger sister. I was humiliated and further convinced me that I was flawed, defective, lacking and inadequate.

I muddled through the next few years, relocating first to NYC and later to Atlanta. On the outside, I appeared to be winning, but on the inside, I was struggling and feeling a constant void in my life. As a result of this void, I felt as if I always had to outperform, overdo, overcommit, over-give and overcompensate to prove myself and that I was worthy, capable, competent, relevant, important, significant, and necessary. I even took on other people's responsibilities and shortcomings to prove I was a good person, a good friend and a good girlfriend. Sadly, I believed that eventually my performance would prove my value and goodness to people and I would no longer have to feel defective, flawed, wrong, or broken. What I did not understand at the time is that our self-worth and value can never be measured by our performance, our doing, or our works. Instead, it is an inner knowing and understanding of who we are and the belief that who we are is enough, adequate, valid and acceptable.

Intellectually, I knew this. I taught it to others. Eventually God made sure I knew it for myself. What I discovered is that life does not require us to prove ourselves. In fact, our very existence is proof that we are worthy, deserving, and good enough. Anything counter to that is an illusion and the result of misperceptions in the mind and painful emotional experiences. For the first time in my life, I got it! There was nothing for me to prove and there never had been. All I ever needed to do was accept that I am enough and approve of myself. My accomplishments and achievements are not what make me enough nor does the lack of them make me *not enough*. My material possessions do not give me value, I give them value. Other people's approval or acceptance of me does not make me worthy, *I* determine that. This revelation has truly changed my life and I now get to just be. I get to be me with no need to prove anything to anyone. No need to hold back and no need to over-give or over-do. No need to explain, justify or apologize. Every day in every way, I get to simply show up as me and the freedom and liberation this has brought me is immeasurable.

Jesus said "they shall know the truth and the truth shall make them free" and the truth is that there is nothing for you or me to prove. You are already approved of by God and by life itself. Your good works do not make you more approved of any more than your mistakes, shortcomings or failures make you less approved. If there are things you desire and wish to change about yourself and your life, change them. Get counseling. Get a life coach. Forgive others and yourself. Make amends where necessary and right any wrongs. Grow, expand and stretch yourself. But do it from a place of knowing you are already approved of and worthy; because you are.

Personal Reflection:

1) In what ways or areas might you be still seeking approval of others?

2) What would it mean for you to really approve of yourself?

3) How would your life change if you knew you had nothing to prove to anyone?

Chapter 5

You Are Already Good Enough

"I Am Enough. I Have Always Been Enough.
I Will Always Be Enough"
~~Unknown

In addition to knowing we have nothing to prove, we must also understand and accept that we are already good enough. Not feeling good enough is one of the most universal core beliefs that exists. Louise Hay actually shared that she has discovered that everyone struggles with this feeling at some point in their lives. Not feeling good enough or constantly feeling inadequate or incomplete is a belief in the illusion that there is something we need to do, become or have in order to measure up. The problem with this, is that even if we were to achieve and obtain those things, it still would not be enough because the reality is that while we may certainly feel inadequate, lacking, incomplete, or broken, I have found that there really is no such thing as not being good enough or what I like to call "enough, enough".

This feeling or belief that we are not good enough usually stems from childhood experiences that may have caused us to feel as if we failed to measure up to someone else's standards. This may be our parents, peers, teachers, coaches and even friends. Whenever I am working with clients in this area, I always ask what will make them good enough. Rarely do they have an answer because quite often they have already exhausted themselves doing one thing after another which still has not worked. The feelings are still there. When someone does respond, the response is often to make a certain amount of money, marry the right person, go to the right school, or earn the right degree. The interesting thing is that many of them have already achieved those things and yet still do not feel good enough and have not yet earned the approval they are seeking. As I stated in an earlier chapter, the reason why external possessions or accomplishments will not work is because we cannot fill an internal void or need with external "stuff". It may appear to work initially, but it will not last and we will find ourselves searching for the next person, place or thing to fill our emotional cups. The truth is, what could you or I possibly ever do, buy or achieve in life to cause us to feel good enough on the outside when we do not feel good enough on the inside? The answer is, nothing. If we do not feel and believe we are good enough within, there is nothing we can do on the outside that will satisfy or remove that feeling. Knowing we are good enough, like everything else we have discussed so far, is an inside job.

What's more intriguing is when we realize that even the questioning or doubting of our worth is often the result of what has been projected onto us by someone else who is trying to fulfill their own internal needs and inadequacies; therefore, the issue is not even ours! I know many people, both personally and professionally, who have spent their whole lives not knowing their worth and trying to live up to someone else's standards of "good enough" whether that is a person, a social group, employer, club, or team. When we decide that we are already good enough and "enough, enough" on the inside and have been since the beginning, we will start to understand that there is no real "standard of measurement". Then we can accept and validate our true internal value and worth.

Several months ago, I was watching an episode of The Real TV Show's "Girl Chat" and they were discussing how girls and women compare themselves with one another and usually end up finding flaws and fault in each other because of some physical characteristic or personality trait. One of the hosts suggested that instead of comparing ourselves to others, we should remind ourselves of our own accomplishments and achievements. I remember wanting to call in at that very moment to say, "No, we are not good enough because of our accomplishments, achievements, accolades, education, certifications, salaries, or material possessions. We are good enough simply because we are!" You and I are a living, breathing extension and expression of God and we were good enough from the exact moment of our conception. We have never had to do, be or acquire anything to qualify, certify or justify that. Sadly, we were taught, and have been believing the wrong thing. This is why I say it is an illusion that has been created in the mind and perpetuated across genders, cultures, races, ethnicities and generations. We are already enough. You are enough. I am enough. This does not mean we cannot or should not set and achieve goals, accomplish great things, make a lot of money, or live a full, wonderful life, but we can do all of that from a place of internal and intrinsic worth and value, and not from a need to measure up because of lack, incompleteness or inadequacy. We can be great and do great things with the knowledge and understanding that we are still enough even without those things, and that to add them to our lives is like adding the dressing to a salad, the glass of wine to a meal, or the dessert after dinner. It just makes things a bit more enjoyable, but it was never meant to be a replacement or substitute for the real thing.

During a radio interview once, I was asked why I felt a lot of people lead off introductions of themselves with a list of their titles and achievements. My response was that we have forgotten how to just be who we are *or* we have never known who we are. Instead, we identify and define ourselves by what we do and we tell ourselves that if we have done enough and accomplished enough, then we have proven that we are good enough and belong. In doing so, we often miss a wonderful opportunity to form deep meaningful connections and relationships because we introduce people to our resumes and not our true, authentic selves. I believe this stems from an internal sense of insecurity, inadequacy, and self-consciousness and we use this to ensure that we measure up and we are seen as "good enough".

According to The Law of Abundance, there is always enough of everything and any lack or scarcity we perceive and experience is in our own minds. You and I are already "enough, enough" and good enough. We are also smart enough, pretty enough, gifted enough, talented enough, special enough, or any other enough. If someone or some experience has convinced us otherwise, then we have to do the work to overcome that erroneous programming and self-limiting belief. As I frequently share with my clients, just because we believe something doesn't make it true, and because it is just a belief, it can be changed. The truth is that we are enough simply because we are, and there is no reason to do more, become more or have more to validate that. We must simply be willing to accept it and then begin living life from this fresh new perspective. When we do not, it can lead to perfectionism.

Perfectionism

Perfectionism is one of the most prevalent issues I see in my therapy practice. Honestly, 95% of the people I work with whom are struggling with depression and anxiety also suffer from perfectionism. First, let me thoroughly define perfectionism, because unfortunately many people who are struggling with it are not even aware of it. People think perfectionism only refers to Obsessive Compulsive Disorder or OCD, but perfectionism goes beyond that. Perfectionism is a pervasive issue of striving for perfection in one's performance, accomplishments, goals, appearance and life. It is a basic belief that we ourselves are somehow inadequate, inherently flawed, incomplete, lacking or defective which generates the constant need to over compensate and make up for those areas of lack. As human beings, we have an innate need to live in balance and harmony, and when we have a belief that we are lacking, there is the tendency to over-compensate and over-correct which often becomes perfectionism. People who suffer from feelings of perfectionism often do not feel good enough or worthy enough and tend to have deep seated feelings of inadequacy and inferiority. Sometimes they are referred to as type A personalities; high-strung overachievers, but at the root of this issue are pervasive feelings of not being good enough. Perfectionists seem to be always striving to achieve some ideal of perfection, misbelieving that if they can become and achieve perfection, it will make up or compensate for their areas of lack and inadequacy. Perfectionists have a need to be in control and they often are very rigid, inflexible and resistant to change. Perfectionists' thought patterns can be very concrete, black or white and all or nothing, and they frequently have trust issues and problems with letting go. I believe that perfectionists frequently suffer from depression because they never seem to be good enough. They may also struggle with high anxiety and varying degrees of self-rejection and even self-hatred, if they are unable to meet and maintain their unrealistic standards of perfection. The illusion in perfectionism is that the person who is trying to reach it never does, and if by some off chance they do, their happiness is usually short-lived because they then set another goal to outperform the last goal. Sadly, the perfectionist is rarely ever satisfied. Their continual reaching and striving keeps them locked in a no-win battle to be perfect despite their inability to accomplish and maintain it. The truth is that perfectionism in this way, cannot be attained. For one thing, it is based on false perceptions of perfection that seem to fluctuate and change each time the individual gets close to it. Secondly, while the perfectionist is often focused on making external changes to achieve perfection, their internal misperception is that they are flawed or inadequate. As a result, they tend to be very performance-driven and results-oriented, often attributing and basing their self-esteem and self-worth on their performance. If their performance meets their standards, they feel successful, accomplished, proud and happy with themselves. If they believe their performance was not good or failed to meet their expectations, they end up feeling worthless and may perceive themselves as a failure. Perfectionists can be harsh, demanding and critical, usually having high expectations of themselves and others. Interestingly, many perfectionists are actually trying to meet someone else's standards of perfection without even realizing it.

Having worked with people of all races, genders, cultures and socioeconomic levels, I have discovered that perfectionists never seem to achieve perfection. When they do appear to reach a preconceived notion of it, they find that their feelings of inadequacy and imperfection are still there, which causes many of them to either give up and sink deep into depression or set more goals until their lives become an endless stream of objectives.

In the book, *Healing Damaged Emotions*, David Seamus informs us of how the perfectionist often struggles in his/her relationship with God. Written from a Christian perspective, David shares that perfectionists believe they even have to perform well enough for God to gain His approval and acceptance, and since God is seen as the ultimate critic and judge, the perfectionist may spend his/her entire life trying to please a God who is impossible to please. They also tend to struggle with being able to feel close to God and receive His love because for the perfectionist, love is often conditional and based on performance and approval. Since the perfectionist feels the need to earn or qualify for God's grace, mercy and love, they often continue to struggle with constant feelings of blame, shame, guilt and failure.

When I am working with clients who are perfectionists, they often dislike when they ask me for a list of activities or exercises they can do to "fix" themselves and their depression, anxiety, low self-esteem or perfectionism and I have to inform them that there is no prescription or formula for them to follow as the real need for healing is with their perception of themselves and not with their performance. Because my response seems too abstract and perfectionists like things to be very concrete and black-and-white, this is often frustrating for them. Instead of facing and confronting their inner feelings of hurt, rejection, inadequacy and insecurity, they continue to seek ways to improve their performance and fix what's wrong with them.

Being what I now refer to as a "Perfectionist in Recovery", I have faced and experienced many of the struggles that perfectionists face, other than OCD. I have struggled to overcome feelings of inadequacy, inferiority and imperfection which have caused me to constantly work to improve and fix myself in my efforts to reach perfection. Because I grew up feeling inherently flawed in a lot of ways and often rejected, I was constantly striving to prove myself worthy of love, approval, and acceptance and make up for some perceived shortcoming in myself. I had all the classic symptoms of perfectionism such as the black-and-white, all-or-nothing thinking, I was rigid and inflexible, hard to please and I set very high standards and expectations for myself and others. I was impatient, demanding and critical of myself and those around me. Feeling like I, the person, was not good enough, I focused on my performance. I tried to do all the right things externally, but I still felt wrong internally. Like a true perfectionist, I just kept trying to find ways to improve and fix myself. I must have read dozens of self-help books, attended church, prayed, fasted, took nutritional supplements, and experimented with various alternative healing methods such as Emotional Freedom Technique (EFT) in my efforts to fix myself. Finally, I began to see that my struggles were not just the result of me being flawed, broken, inferior or inadequate and I was not being punished for something I had done in the past. It was then that I began to understand that perfection was never God's plan or requirement for me or anyone else. Our real journey is about becoming whole, not perfect. As I continued to pray and seek guidance, the more the truth unfolded within me. I realized that all of the ways I had been viewing myself and the world around me was what was flawed, not me. My limiting beliefs and misguided thoughts about myself were what needed adjusting instead of me needing to be fixed. I discovered that being good enough, worthy, acceptable and deserving were inside jobs and could only come from inside of me. The approval I had been so earnestly seeking outside of myself could only be found within me, and the validation I was striving for would never be fulfilled or satisfied externally. I realized that healing and wholeness begin and end with me. It doesn't really matter what I needed and didn't receive from other people, or which of my emotional needs were unmet. What really matters is what I am willing to give and provide for myself. This does not mean I don't value other people's thoughts, ideas and opinions of me, but I no longer base my self-esteem, self-image and self-worth on anyone else but me. How I feel about me and how I see me is what makes the difference. It is what qualifies me and validates me and I get now that I never had anything to prove to anyone. I accept that God loves me and His love is not based on my performance or ability, but on me the individual and I no longer have to earn or qualify for it. God's love and acceptance is freely given and my only requirement is to receive it. Once I discovered this, my whole perspective towards life, God and myself began to change. I became less dependent and affected by what other people they thought of me and I felt free to be myself without explanation, justification or apology.

My life continues to evolve and I continue to learn, grow, and expand from all of my experiences, and not just my successes and achievements. That, for me, is perfect. If you struggle with perfectionism, please know and accept that you are already good enough and there is nothing you need to do, have, or become to prove or validate that.

Personal Reflection:

1) What would be different if you knew without a doubt that you were good enough?

2) How would you interact with others? How would you feel?

3) Do you feel the need to be perfect or appear perfect? If so, why and what has this cost you?

Chapter 6

Be True to Yourself

"To Thine Own Self Be True"
~~William Shakespeare

I remember once hearing Oprah Winfrey speak about how she started out in news trying to emulate Barbara Walters. Oprah admitted that she was so busy trying to be like Barbara one day that she mispronounced a relatively easy word. From that day on, she stopped trying to be Barbara and decided to be Oprah and the results of that enlightened decision are well-known throughout the world. Oprah has gone on to excel in daytime television and acting roles. She has written books, launched her own magazine and two television networks: OWN and Oxygen. She bought into a satellite radio station and has produced movies, TV shows, delivered keynote speaking addresses and even opened a school for girls in Africa. She has interviewed some of the most influential people in the world from celebrities and royalty to everyday heroes. All because she decided to be true to who she is. It certainly makes you think of all that we might be capable of if we poured 100% of our efforts into simply being ourselves instead of worrying, competing, and comparing ourselves to others or trying to imitate, emulate, or duplicate someone else. When I ran track in high school, my coach would caution us against looking at our competitors because she said it would slow us down and even a fraction of a second could cause us to win or lose the race. The truth is that we are only required to be who we are and our only competition is us. You and I are equipped to handle the challenges we will face in our own lives, but we are not equipped to handle those in someone else's life. I like to say I am anointed for my battles, but someone else's battles may kill me. In my book, *Why Am I Still Single*, I even shared that women should never covet someone else's husband because of how he treats his wife, because what may be great for her may "suck" for them. Even the medicines and supplements we take may cause us to thrive and be in good health while they might cause someone else to become sick and die.

The goal for all of us is to become the most authentic and genuine version of ourselves and to do the work necessary to live our own best lives. To do so, we must be willing to overcome our fears and insecurities and face ourselves openly and honestly with genuine love, compassion, acceptance and understanding. We must practice self-love, self-acceptance, and self-approval. Authentic living is when our words and actions are congruent with our beliefs and values, and when we are being who we are rather than who we feel we should be or who we have been told we are. Authenticity is similar to integrity in that we show up as who we are regardless of who we are around or the circumstances we are in. This allows people to be able to trust us because they know we won't change with the tides. It is not always easy to walk, speak, stand and live in authenticity, but it is always worth it. Sometimes, we may not want to speak our truth out of fear that it will hurt someone's feelings or cause distress, but in order to live an authentic life that is true to who we are, we must be willing to speak the truth even when it's not easy and stand on our values even if we have to stand alone. Living authentically means we may have to be vulnerable and transparent even when we know that doing so may cause us to feel scared, exposed to judgment, criticism and embarrassment, or rejection. It means no longer hiding who we are or changing who we are to please others or be more acceptable.

I once read a quote by Dr. Wayne Dyer that said "You cannot fail at being yourself." At the time, I did not fully understand what it meant, but in time it started to make perfect sense. All I can ever be is me and I can never fail at that unless I try to imitate and duplicate someone else. Being me is easy and it comes natural to me.

I once had a client share with me that she had been asked to speak on a huge platform and felt somewhat uneasy because she had not gone to college and was unsure if she should change her "down-to-earth" style of speaking in order to appear more educated and professional. I advised her to be true to her own style of speaking because there are people who will resonates with that. Trying to be something else would be unnatural to her and cause her to feel even more anxiety and distress. She agreed and later told me she nailed it!

Personally, I am still on my journey of living more authentically and I am committed to growing and evolving even when it is not easy or comfortable. Yes, it is a daily process of rooting out what is not genuinely me and what no longer serves me. I have had to end relationships with people, break patterns of unhealthy behavior and admit some hard truths to myself, but in the end, it is well worth it for me to get to know, love, accept, validate and embrace the amazing person that is me. I invite you to do the same.

It may not always be easy to be true to ourselves, especially in a time when there are so many messages telling us what to think, how to speak, what to buy, where to travel, how to shop and what to wear. Sometimes, we will have to go against the grain and do our own thing. Do not be afraid to be a trendsetter and honor your own unique style. It is you and it comes easy to you. Remember, you cannot fail at being yourself.

Personal Reflection:

1) What does it mean for you to just be you and to be true to you?

2) What it is that you bring to the table that is like no one else?

3) What will it require for you to live a genuine, authentic life? What or who will you have to give up or let go of?

4) What courageous conversations will you need to have?

Chapter 7

It's Okay to Be Different

"But mommy, who said it has to match?"
~~My daughter, Morgan Geathers

My six-year-old daughter taught me one of my most important life lessons when she dressed herself one day in unmatching colors and patterns and I made the comment, "Sweetie, that doesn't match". In her own little voice of independence, she said "Mommy it doesn't have to". As innocent and sweet as that interchange was, my daughter taught me during that moment that it is okay not to match colors and patterns, but even more importantly, we must be allowed to express ourselves in our own unique way. When my daughter said "it doesn't have to match", she was also saying 'who said it has to look the same way or even a certain way?' Who made up these rules of sameness and conformity that we all seem to accept and follow automatically? Who says it has to match?

Growing up in a small conservative town in SC, I was constantly faced with feeling the need to follow the rules and conform to socially acceptable norms and trends. The difficult part for me is that I was anything but "the norm". I have always been a free thinker, an innovator and a trendsetter even before I knew what to call it. If everyone else said let's paint the sign red, I was thinking, 'how about purple with stripes.' Being unique, innovative and free was not always encouraged in my family or in my community and I learned very quickly that I either had to conform to the norm or run the risk of being teased and possibly ostracized for daring to be different. Luckily for me, I was also intelligent and attractive so I used those attributes to fit in and blend. Perhaps the only time I saw sparks of my creativity was during my high school talent show or times when I would push the limits with my outfits until some "well-meaning person" decided to point out that what I was wearing didn't match or make fashion sense. At that point, I would shrink a little bit farther into myself until the next time I got up the courage to be different. I remained in this pattern of acceptable behavior and trying to fit in throughout high school and college. After graduating, I moved to Brooklyn, NY and finally it seemed I had found a place that was as eclectic, weird, innovative and different as me. I loved places like Soho and The Village and how open and free New Yorkers appeared to be. I was intrigued by all the different races of people, languages and customs. I had friends who spoke both Mandarin and Cantonese, my doctor was Haitian and my dentist was Jewish. I loved New York and I felt freer than I ever had. I could be me without apology. Finally, after a few years, I decided to relocate back to the south to be closer to my family and I moved to Atlanta. While Atlanta wasn't NYC, it was still a step above where I had grown up. After a year, I moved back home only to find that not much had changed in the years I had been gone. It was still the same conservative, small town it had always been and I was still an African-American female trying to find my place in it. Slowly but surely, I began to feel my newfound freedom of expression and uniqueness morphing right back into a nice, socially acceptable bubble. I spent the next few years trying to conform. I can remember wanting to wear my hair a certain way and being told it was not professional enough. I remember having to choose certain outfits that did not cause me to stand out too much. On the outside, I appeared to fit in and blend, but inside, a part of me was dying. Dying to be free and dying to be me. However, I did not have the courage then that I have now, so I did what was safe and hid the real me. Finally, in 2012, I married a man who fully accepted me for me and didn't ask or expect me to change a thing! I had quit my full-time job and was working for myself in my own private practice. What's crazy is that even though I was self-employed, I would still go to lunch and stay for exactly an hour until one day it hit me that I was no longer in a box or having to follow other people's rules. It was then that I began to regain my sense of freedom and my creativity returned full force. I began to think outside of the box intentionally!

Over the next several years, I continued to work with clients and do my own inner work to be free. I realized and accepted that I had been born to be different, unique, and creative. I was never meant to fit in. When I have clients struggling with the same thing, I share my own wisdom and understanding and watch as client after client reconnects with their true selves and experiences a freedom they have either long forgotten or never experienced. I understood that I was never meant to blend and in fact, I was born to stand out and be set apart. Blending requires us to lose a sense of ourselves and our own individuality and uniqueness. I discovered that by not blending in, I got to be different, follow my own rules, set my own trends, and march to the beat of my own drum. At this stage of life, I have begun to celebrate my uniqueness instead of hiding it or apologizing for it. I now wear statements that boldly express my individuality such as my tee shirt that says **Extra,** or my social media post that says "I have absolutely no desire to fit in". I can remember how I would shrink whenever someone called me extra, and now I openly express it and embrace it. I am no longer a round peg trying to fit into a square hole. I am me and I have always been a trailblazer, a free thinker, and a pioneer. I am committed to living my life as authentically as I can and I also encourage my children to think freely and to be okay with who they are even when it doesn't blend or fit. "So, thank you baby girl, you were right, it doesn't have to match and neither do we!"

Personal Reflection:

1) Are you trying to fit in with someone else's idea of who or what you should be or do? If so, how can you begin to reclaim your sense of freedom and individuality?

2) Do you feel free to be your own person, regardless of who disagrees or disapproves of you?

3) What would happen if you embraced your unique self and dared to be different?

4) Have you squashed your creativity in efforts to fit and blend?

Chapter 8

The Unseen

"Don't let what you see make you forget what I said"
~~ God

In 2019, I did a six-week segment on my talk radio show on the subject of trust. My listeners were so intrigued by these discussions that I was frequently asked about leading workshops and classes to help people identify, address and overcome their trust issues. It was then that I began to truly understand the importance of trust, not just as a value or a virtue, but as an essential element that must be included in any relationship we have, even the one we have with ourselves. I learned that when trust is missing, it will most certainly hinder our ability to open ourselves up to other people and the process of life itself. Without trust, we may struggle in our romantic and other interpersonal relationships and we may also struggle to trust God or a Higher Power. We may fail to trust authority figures such as our employers, healthcare professionals and public officials; we may not even trust our own bodies to the point of fearing that we may have some hidden disease or ailment. The truth is that while it may not be easy or simple, trust is necessary in order for us to have healthy relationships and without it, we may wrestle with frequent insecurities, fears, doubts, jealousy and suspicion.

During my deep dive into the subject of trust, I discovered that almost everything we do and experience in life essentially boils down to the element of trust. Trust is defined as a belief in the truth, reliability, ability, or strength of someone or something and is synonymous with faith, confidence and belief. According to German-

American psychologist, Erik Erikson, trust is developed in the first stage of life between birth and eighteen months of age when an infant is dependent upon their parents and caregivers to respond to their needs for food, care, attention, and affection. If the responses are reliable and consistent, the infant learns that it is safe to trust others and trust that his/her needs will be met. When this does not happen or it happens inconsistently, the infant develops mistrust and may adopt the belief that the people in their lives will not meet their physical and emotional needs. The infant may also conclude that he/she is not wanted, welcome or important based on the presence or lack of responses they receive. Consequently, if the mistrust is not resolved in childhood, the infant grows into an adult who continues to carry these trust issues into every relationship and life experience they have, making it difficult to develop true intimacy and connectedness.

Just as important as it is to learn to trust others and the world around us, I now know that it is equally, if not more important that we learn to trust ourselves. Sadly, most of us were never taught to trust ourselves and still may not know how to do so. Trusting ourselves can also help us avoid dangerous or bad situations, including unhealthy relationships.

As children, we were taught to trust our parents, teachers, coaches, etc., but we are rarely taught or advised to trust ourselves. Self-trust is the willingness and the ability to trust our own decisions, judgments, ideas, insights, internal urges, gut instincts and intuition. Self-trust also means being willing to protect ourselves, make ourselves a priority in our own lives, respect and honor ourselves, and approve, affirm and validate who we really are. In my first book, I talk about how we often overlook obvious warning signs in relationships in our desire to trust someone and take them at their word even if there is significant evidence to the contrary. For example, we may truly believe or "know" someone is being dishonest with us, but we will abandon that still, small voice on the inside because we do not want to offend them, hurt their feelings or cause problems in the relationship. Instead, we will go against ourselves and put our trust in the other person, all the while knowing we should be cautious or examine the situation more closely. Sadly, sometimes our need to belong and be loved may outweigh our willingness to self-protect. I have known many people, personally and professionally, who have completely abandoned the responsibility of self-trust and placed all of their expectations in another person, only to spend their time wishing, hoping and praying that the other person will keep their word and turn out to be who they appear to be. The truth of the matter is that self-trust and self-care are our responsibility and even though we may still end up hurt, cheated on, lied to and mistreated, we will at least not have the added guilt of knowing something was off and willingly choosing to ignore our own intuition.

Early on in my relationship with my husband, I was wrestling with my own trust issues that seemed to have been there for as long as I could remember. Despite my husband (who was my boyfriend at the time) giving me no reason to distrust him whatsoever, I still felt things were too good to be true and that I should not let my guard down. The funny thing is he seemed to have no trouble trusting me. I mean the reality is that I knew I was faithful, but I also knew he had no way of knowing that for sure. One day I asked him how he could be so trusting of me. His response left me speechless and singlehandedly changed my whole perspective on self-trust. He said, "Because I trust me and I trust me not to allow myself to be disrespected, taken advantage of, lied to or cheated on so if that happens, I trust me to do what is necessary to protect myself". "Wow", I remember thinking, "How secure it must feel to trust yourself to that extent." Because of my painful life experiences, I had never learned to trust me or protect me; therefore, I constantly worried about whether I could trust other people and usually approached people from a position of *not* trusting them and an expectation that at some point, they would disappoint me. After hearing my husband's response and finally getting it internally, I began the process of learning to trust me and I started off by making some promises to myself. I promised to walk in truth and integrity; I promised to always protect my heart, but not hide my heart; I promised to value me and put me first; I promised to trust my instincts and my own internal voice; I promised to honor me, respect me and fill my own love tank so that I would never be tempted to sell myself out for anyone else's benefit, approval, or acceptance.

While I do believe there is wisdom in seeking advice and wise counsel from others, I do not feel we should use that as an excuse to justify or negate our own internal knowing, or our responsibility to ourselves. When we begin to trust in ourselves and our own internal guidance system (which is always readily available to us), we learn to live from a place of authenticity, completeness, wholeness and fulfillment and we will find that it is easier to trust God, others, and the world around us. This will also help us to be able to trust the process of life and we will no longer have to live from a place of defensiveness and guardedness. We can begin to believe that life is for us and that even our setbacks, disappointments, heartbreaks, rejections, etc. will eventually work out for our good. Now that I have learned to trust me and keep my promises to myself, I operate from a much more secure space and state of being. While I do not go into every new relationship or interaction blindly trusting, I also do not enter into them *distrusting*. I look at it as entering the pool from the shallow end and gradually progressing to the deep end, rather than automatically diving into the deep end or sitting on the sidelines, not getting in at all. As a result, I have found it easier to trust because I can and do trust me and even though I am aware that this will not prevent me from all emotional, physical, or relational injury, I am comfortable in knowing that I can handle whatever comes my way. You too can grow in trust. Trust in God or your Higher Power, trust in others, trust in the process and trust in yourself.

You Gotta Have Faith

This chapter on trust and faith was one of the hardest for me to write, not because I didn't know what to say, but because I knew I had to dive deep in a way that would be truly transformational, practical and applicable. I also knew that I could not fluff the material nor could I simply repeat the definitions of trust and faith from a religious or philosophical perspective. Not only did I want the reader to gain a real life understanding of these two concepts, I wanted to develop my own revelational understanding so I could speak from a genuine, authentic place.

This entire book, Epiphany, is a portrait of my growth and evolution over the past few years and none of it would mean anything if I did not learn to define, apply and live by faith. Trust and faith are synonymous which means it is hard to define one without the other and I believe it is almost impossible to have one without the other because of their interdependence on one another. In order to have faith, you must trust and in order to trust, you must have faith. I can attest to the fact that because I struggled with trust, I also struggled with faith. I now believe that we are born with faith and trust. In actuality, the miracle of birth itself is not of our own doing, and is a testament of faith and trust beyond our need for understanding or explanation. In essence, there is no need *to* trust or *to* have faith, there just is trust and there just is faith; therefore, we have no need to have faith per se, because we are faith. Faith and trust along with love and joy are the very essence of who and what we are made of, which is why we struggle in their absence. When there is an absence of joy, we suffer from depression or general unhappiness. When there is an absence of love, we suffer from hatred, bitterness, blame, resentment, fear, anger, guilt, and shame. In the absence of trust, we struggle with suspicion, fear, guardedness, and insecurity and in the absence of faith, we feel exposed, unprotected, unsafe, uncovered, and alone. I believe that our natural state is trust, love, joy and faith and it feels unnatural when we do not understand and accept this.

"Now faith, is the substance (physical matter) of things hoped for and the evidence (proof) of things not seen". I have read and heard this scripture my entire life, but the epiphany I gained in writing this chapter goes beyond any of my previous knowledge, understanding or insight. What I now know for sure is that faith is not dependent or contingent upon physical evidence, faith *is* the evidence. Faith is the proof that what we are believing for, already exists. It is not coming, if and when God decides to answer our prayers, faith is the actual proof of its NOW existence. It is the substance of what we hope for and the word substance is defined as physical, tangible matter. That means that what we hope for already exists in a physical and tangible form and the reason we may not see it yet is simply a matter of divine timing or a lack of awareness. I believe we struggle with faith because we think of faith as something conceptual and that we need to get, gain, acquire or develop it, which is actually a belief in the absence of faith rather than the presence of it. Then we try and get it from outside of us without realizing that faith is already on the inside of us waiting to be recognized and activated. When we accept faith as a part of who and what we are, then we know by its very definition that faith is the evidence and the substance (the proof and the physical matter) of that which we hope. So, the truth is that you and I were not meant to simply have faith, we were meant to discover the faith which may be lying dormant inside of us waiting for us to activate it. Need faith to start a new business? Activate it. Need faith to overcome a challenge? Activate it. Need faith to heal from an affliction? Activate it. The word 'activate' means to turn on, energize and set in motion, and the exact moment that we choose to activate our faith, it becomes a powerful force that begins to set in motion the circumstances, conditions, and outcomes that we eventually experience in our lives.

In order to activate and live our faith, we must also be willing to trust in the unseen and because we have been taught to rely so heavily on our physical senses, it is difficult for us to have faith in what we cannot visibly see. If we cannot see, hear, taste, touch or smell something, we consider it to be invisible and therefore, unreal. When you really think about it, we put faith in things that are not real all the time such as electricity, gravity, and oxygen. We have faith that our cars are going to start when we turn the key or press the ignition. We have faith that the lights will come on when we flip a switch. In fact, our expectation is so strong that we are actually surprised when these things do not work and just as we may not fully understand why or how electricity works but still choose to live by it, we may not always fully understand how and why faith works in order to live by it.

What's even more interesting to me is that as children, faith seems to come naturally to us. As children, we were not so quick to question everything and we were much more willing to believe in what we could not see. We believed in fairies, mermaids and unicorns even though we never laid eyes on them. We believed in talking mice, that there was a pot of gold at the end of the rainbow and that magic carpets really could fly. Unfortunately, because of certain life experiences, we start to bury our open, trusting, faithful nature and over time, we become suspicious, untrusting and guarded. When I was young, I believed that anything was possible and I saw the absolute best in people. Inherently, I already knew that part of my purpose on earth was to help people see the best in themselves and become the best they could be. Sadly, this also led me to come in contact with people who viewed my open, trusting nature as an opportunity to take advantage of me. As a result, I blamed myself for being too open and too trusting and I built emotional walls around myself to keep me safe. Instead of seeing the best in people, I began seeing everyone as a potential threat and I decided that people could not be trusted and the world was not a safe place. This made it almost impossible for me to have faith and this is also why many people struggle with faith. Faith, like trust, usually gets damaged in childhood or adolescence. Even though there may be events that occur later in life, the wounds that we endure in childhood seem to cut the deepest and have lasting, long term effects. The good news is that faith can be restored and we can learn to trust again. We can reignite that childlike faith and trust that came so naturally to us, and we can surrender the need to know "how and why". In reality, we may never know or understand how or why, which is when we have to lean not on our own understanding. Faith requires us to let go and to accept we will not always be able to predict or control the process or the outcome, but we can trust that the outcome that shows up is for our ultimate good. Faith may also require us to be able to separate truth from facts. Facts change, truth is immutable. Lastly, faith requires us to believe. Believe in good, believe in ourselves and believe that there is a power in the universe that is for us and wants us to win even when we cannot and do not see it.

In the 2020 box office movie, *The Invisible Man*, there is a scene where the main character throws paint onto the invisible man and reveals his physical form. For some reason, I did not have a full understanding of what invisible meant, because I remember my husband explaining to me that being invisible did not mean he wasn't there, it just meant that he could not be seen. How often do we doubt whether something is there because we cannot see it? I am so grateful that God has not only given us physical sight, but He has also given us spiritual sight that allows us to see beyond the physical, material world into the invisible world which exists even if we cannot see it. Faith is the substance/physical matter of what we hope for and our evidence/proof of what is unseen. When we truly embrace this and begin to trust in the inevitability of the unseen, we discover infinite possibilities and opportunities. The unseen is where our divine health and healing is; the unseen is where our ideal, fulfilling relationships are and where our enriching life experiences reside. The unseen is where our treasures are stored and where the wealth and abundance that is our birthrights is kept. The unseen is where our untapped potential lies along with our ability to transcend, transform and transmute the physical world. The unseen is not unreal or nonexistent, it is merely invisible to the physical eye. It is the underlying factor that allows everything we do see and experience to be and become. This is why we must walk by faith and not by sight and why we are encouraged to "fix our eyes not on what is seen, but what is unseen".

Personal Reflection:

1) What if you were able to truly trust yourself without a doubt?

2) How would developing your ability to trust others change your relationships?

3) How would completely trusting God/Higher Power enhance your life?

4) How can activating your faith improve your life? Will it cause you to worry less and have less anxiety?

5) Is there an area of your life where you need to activate faith right now?'

Chapter 9

When You Believe

"You don't become what you want,
you become what you believe"
~~Oprah Winfrey

Anyone who has ever aspired to do anything great or to simply excel beyond their current state of being, will at some point have to examine their beliefs about themselves and decide what they believe is possible. I am no different. I now understand the absolute importance of believing and I understand how my beliefs about myself, God, other people and the world have affected me throughout my life and continue to influence every aspect of my existence.

By definition, a belief (noun) is defined as the acceptance that a statement is true or that someone or something exists. A belief is further defined as trust, faith and confidence in someone or something. We may have religious or spiritual beliefs in addition to beliefs that are cultural, political, generational, geographical, and environmental. We also have beliefs about relationships, parenting, finances, health, food, medicine, other people, and we even have beliefs about ourselves. In fact, these beliefs we have about ourselves shape and determine the course and the conditions of our lives. If we believe ourselves to be competent, capable, worthy and deserving of good things, then we will most likely see evidence of that in our lives. Likewise, if we believe ourselves to be inadequate, worthless, lacking, broken, or incompetent, then we will also see evidence of that in our lives. The reality is that whatever we believe about ourselves and about the world will create our sense of reality and directly affect what we experience.

In the book, *You'll See it When You Believe It,* by Dr. Wayne Dyer, he explains that what we see is not necessarily a reality, but an outward reflection of our inner beliefs. I now understand that our inner world is what we see projected onto our outer world. As Within, So Without. If there is a condition in our lives that we want to change or eliminate, then it is our beliefs that must be examined and changed rather than the condition itself since the condition is merely a reflection of the belief. Essentially, we must address the source of our issues and beliefs rather than trying to address the conditions. We often see this approach in Eastern medicine which focuses on identifying the source of an ailment, condition or disease rather than simply treating the symptoms of it. This is also my approach in therapy. My clients are often surprised when I tell them I am less concerned about their symptoms of depression, anxiety, sadness, or anger, etc. than I am with identifying the source of it. I work with them identify their underlying beliefs about themselves, others and the world, and then help them work to shift those beliefs that may be contributing to their dis-ease and limiting their happiness and success. Once we address the source of their distress and discomfort, the symptoms begin to alleviate themselves which is why 95% of my clients do not return to me to address the same issue once they have completed their treatment.

I also did a four-week series on my radio show on Belief where I discussed the importance of our beliefs and also the importance of believing in ourselves and our abilities. I shared the differences between empowering beliefs and self-limiting beliefs. Empowering beliefs are beliefs that empower us and give us confidence and faith in our abilities and who we are. Empowering beliefs may be things such as "I am capable, I am important, I am worthy, I am deserving, I belong, I am loved, or I am wanted". Self-limiting beliefs are beliefs that limit us such as "I am not good

enough, I am not worthy, I am not lovable, or I am not important".
During that four-week series on my radio show, I shared examples of
how belief had propelled ordinary people beyond their limitations as
in the case of Roger Bannister who broke the four-minute mile
barrier in 1954. Prior to that, people believed it was humanly
impossible to run a four-minute mile until Roger broke through that
collective limiting belief. It is said that his record only lasted 46 days
because once people knew it was possible, others began to regularly
run a mile in under four minutes. This is just one example of the
power of our beliefs.

If our beliefs are so powerful, how are they formed? Some
believe that we are born without preconceived beliefs and that our
beliefs are formed as a result of our experiences, inferences and
conclusions. I believe our beliefs are also influenced by our gender,
culture, age, race, place of birth and even the circumstances
surrounding our birth. These and other factors are what compel us to
form beliefs that are self-affirming or self-limiting. The good news is
that beliefs can be changed and as I stated in an earlier chapter, just
because we believe something doesn't make it true, even if it appears,
sounds or feels true. We have the power and the ability to change our
self-limiting, negative beliefs to beliefs that are self-affirming and
empowering. It may not be easy, but it's possible and because our
beliefs become the reality that we eventually experience, it is critical
that we examine our beliefs, identify those that are no longer serving
us and do the necessary work to shift and transform them.

I can genuinely say that I have worked hard to overcome the
limiting beliefs in my life that were the result of my own painful life
experiences along with the collective beliefs of my family, peers,
society and culture. I have overcome many of the negative beliefs I
had about myself, my body, my life, my race and even my gender. I
have overcome beliefs about other people which also led to
judgments and assumptions about other people. If my beliefs
determine what I become and what kind of life I live, then I intend to

develop and maintain those that cause me to feel good, think positively and enjoy my life to the fullest. I have done the work to relinquish the mental programming and conditioning that is no longer relevant or necessary and I have been adopting beliefs that better serve me. In addition to developing self-affirming beliefs *about* myself, I have also had to learn to believe (verb) *in* myself. Because I understand the power that comes from believing in ourselves, I also know the power it has to unlock forces within us that make the impossible possible. Furthermore, I understand the importance of believing in God and the unseen so that even when I cannot or do not see things happening, I can choose to believe and have faith that they will eventually show up. Remember, as a child we had no preconceived beliefs until life got its hands on us, and we can choose to shift our limiting beliefs to those that are more self-affirming and that better serve who and where we are NOW.

Personal Reflection:

1) Make a list of your own limiting beliefs.

2) How have these beliefs held you back?

3) What are some ways you can begin to shift your limiting beliefs to empowering beliefs?

4) What would it mean for you to really believe in yourself?

Chapter 10

See Beyond the Obvious

"Vision is the art of seeing what is invisible to others"
~~Jonathan Swift

In 2005, I visited a friend in Los Angeles, California and noticed a poster board she had taped to the wall of her bedroom. It had pictures and positive affirmations pasted onto it. Intrigued, I asked her what it was and she told me it was a vision board. I had never heard of vision boards before, but I wanted to know more. When I returned home a few days later, I started researching vision boards online and decided to host my own vision board party in my home. There were nine women spread throughout the downstairs of my house and we spent the entire afternoon going through magazines, cutting out images and pasting them onto our boards. For the next several years, I continued creating my own vision boards every year and hosting vision board parties so I could teach others how to create them and the importance of having one. Time and again, people who attended my workshops shared testimonies of things that had manifested in their lives from wedding engagements, new homes, international travel, promotions and articles being published in national journals. Perhaps the biggest success story came from my own sister who created one with a photo representing her desire to have a baby. My sister had struggled with infertility for years and had at one time given up on having a child of her own. I encouraged her to put the photo on her vision board and years later, my sister became pregnant and gave birth to a healthy baby boy. I had also placed a photo on own my vision board in 2011 of a family of four including a wife, husband, son and daughter. At the time, I was engaged and we already had a two-year old son. We got married in September of 2012 and by October, I was pregnant with a daughter who was born the following June. In short, vision boards work, and I have witnessed amazing things continuing to manifest from vision boards I created years ago. After the Gabby Douglas story aired and highlighted her family's use of vision boards or dream boards, people everywhere began creating their own and enjoying similar successes.

What I want to focus on in this chapter however is not just the creation of a vision board, but the importance of having a vision and being a person of vision. Vision is more than simply having the physical faculty of sight. In fact, having sight does not automatically mean you have vision. There are many people who have physical sight, but lack vision and many unsighted people who have incredible vision. A person with vision is someone who is able to see beyond the images captured by their physical eyesight and recognize the potential of something way before it manifests and becomes the thing envisioned. The word envision means to visualize, imagine and picture a future possibility. Because the mind constructs things in images and pictures rather than words, we can use our minds to envision the types of relationships we desire, the ideal job or career path, and even material items we would love to own such as homes, cars and money through our ability to envision, imagine and visualize.

I have always been a person of vision and what many people would call a visionary. I have always seen people and things for what they could be rather than just what was presented to me. As a child, I was always daydreaming and using my mind to imagine different scenarios and experiences. At five, I discovered my love for reading and became fascinated with how someone could use words to create images in my mind and even transport me to distant, faraway places without me ever leaving my house. My first year after graduation from college, I created and hosted a self-esteem pageant for teenaged girls in my hometown and discovered that I could create and plan events from ideas in my mind. I would literally sit in my bedroom and see things play out in my head as if it was on a movie screen. I never thought much of this ability because it was just second nature to me, but after studying the Law of Attraction and discovering the importance of vision and imagination, I now know that this imaging faculty that has been there throughout my entire life is an amazing gift. Whether it's creating events, being a makeup artist for twelve years, building and renovating homes or my current work as a psychotherapist, life coach and speaker, my life path is that of one who sees beyond the surface and envisions what can be and what is possible for myself and other people. I can look at an empty lot and see a home or a building sitting on it. I look at a blank computer screen and see an unwritten story waiting to be told. I can look at a person suffering with low self-esteem and see a powerful individual capable of amazing things. I often share with my clients that no matter how hopeless things may seem, I always maintain an image of their healing as a finished product rather than simply focusing on the issues and challenges at hand. By seeing the end from the beginning, I am able to help them map out a process for reaching it.

My ability to use my imagination, vision and insight has also provided me with the skills and the tools necessary for me to create the life of my dreams even though I am just now fully discovering this incredible power. Being able to imagine, envision and visualize is our mind's ability to create and manifest the things we desire to be, do and have in life. For a greater part of my life, I did not think much about my daydreaming or my imagination being such a valuable asset. I just knew it was something I did that I enjoyed, and because of my lack of knowledge and understanding, I spent a lot of time, energy and money doing things the hard way. I had not learned to tap into my mind's amazing power to create and attract the things I wanted. Actually, I was using my mind's power to attract the things I did *not* want, and I could not understand why I continued to manifest those things despite my best efforts to change them.

By now, if you are familiar with The Secret and The Law of Attraction (LOA), then you have heard that our thoughts and feelings are attracting things into our lives or pushing things out of our lives. Whether we believe in the LOA or not, we are always attracting, but most of us are attracting what we don't want rather than what we do want. For example, you may not want to be alone, but instead of seeing yourself with a loving partner, you focus on your fear of being alone which attracts more aloneness. Despite our best goals and intentions to attract a healthy relationship, if we are focusing more on the absence of it rather than the presence of it, we will continue to experience the absence. According to the LOA, we attract what we are and what we focus on expands. This is why gratitude is such an important quality to imbibe, because it keeps us focused on what we do have which attracts more for us to be grateful for. In my Keys to Manifesting Boot Camp, one of my students realized the importance of this in regards to her son who had been seriously injured in a car accident. Each time she talked about her desire for him to get better and be restored to full health, she would tell me what he could no longer do. I then advised her to begin focusing all her attention on what he could do and what he had left, instead of on what he had lost. I also encouraged her to get a picture of him before the accident and envision him being fully restored. Within thirty days, she reached out to inform me that her son had started working part-time and was feeling better than ever. It wasn't magic. It wasn't mystery. It was vision. Once she held onto it steadfastly in her mind, it had to manifest and become a reality. You too can begin to harness the power of your imagination and the truth is you are already attracting things, so be willing to shift your focus off of what you do not want and onto what you do.

Personal Reflection:

1) What is it you want to be, do and have?

2) Can you envision your ideal life?

3) What is the life that would WOW you?

Chapter 11

Debt Free
The Power of Forgiving & Letting Go

"To err is human: to forgive, divine."
Author Unknown

In this day and age, most of us have heard of the power of forgiveness, whether at church, from our parents or through our own personal experiences. Even though we may be familiar with the concept of forgiveness, we may still struggle with understanding why we should forgive and how to forgive. When you think about it, it can feel unnatural to forgive someone who has wronged us because we have an innate need for self-protection. Honestly, every living thing on the planet has a built-in defense mechanism; from the skunk to the porcupine, the bee, the snake and yes even human beings. Survival is a basic primal instinct, so to react against an attack or an offense is natural to us. To not react or to react by forgiving the attack or offense can feel unnatural. That is, until we really understand what forgiveness is and what it isn't.

I am blessed to have friends in my life who forgive easily. It seems that no matter what is done to them or how bad it was, they will forgive in a heartbeat. I admire that, especially because forgiveness is not something that has come easily to me. I can admit that I have always seen the importance of it., but it seemed that despite how hard I tried, my feelings of anger and resentment remained, which made forgiveness almost impossible. The truth of the matter is that I wasn't always this way. When I was younger, I would forgive someone at the drop of a dime. I honestly believed in second chances and that everyone was capable of making mistakes.

This made forgiving people easy; however, over time my forgiving nature seemed to invite one infraction after another and it seemed that no matter how good I tried to be or however loving and understanding, someone always seemed to mistake my kindness for weakness and take advantage of me. This is when I began to withhold forgiveness, thinking this would somehow prevent me from being injured. I tried to overlook things and let things go, but after every new betrayal, deception, offense, and heartbreak, I retreated further and further behind my emotional walls. Sadly, not only did those walls not prevent me from future harm, they also kept people out and simultaneously, kept me locked in. The other reason I think forgiveness became so difficult for me was because I had not stood up for or defended myself against any of my sexual perpetrators. In fact, I had kept quiet about all of it in my efforts to shoulder the burdens of it by myself. I would watch as they continued on as if nothing happened, and even smile at me as if we were friends. This infuriated me and it also caused me to feel stupid and weak. Forgive them? No way.

It wasn't until God really revealed to me the purpose and power of forgiveness that I began to make a conscious effort to let go and release people I had been holding captive. That's the thing about unforgiveness; it is like we are still holding people accountable to us and therefore it is like we have them locked in an emotional prison, not even realizing that we are locked away as well. When I started to understand that forgiveness was not a passive thing and that it did not make me weak, I commenced the process of forgiving everyone for everything, including me. No longer was I willing to justify, defend or rationalize my right to stay angry, resentful or vengeful to prove why I was right and they were wrong. In the chapter on love, I share how emotions vibrate and resonate at specific frequencies and also have the ability to lower our body's frequency to the same level of the emotion. When we are vibrating at lower levels by harboring hatred, guilt, bitterness and resentment, we become susceptible to every virus, bacteria, disease and condition that is also vibrating on that same level. So, I knew that unforgiveness was like a cancer running rampant in the cells of my mind and body and if I did not do something soon, it would destroy my health, my happiness and eventually my life. I decided then that no one deserved to have that kind of power over me; literally the power of life and death. I made a list of every offense, infraction, insult, deception, and attack that I had ever experienced and began the process of letting them go, one by one. It was difficult at first and some of them required me to repeat the process several times, but eventually it got easier. I also had to acknowledge and address the hurt and sadness that was underlying the anger and resentment so I could fully resolve it. This was an emotional, painful process, but in the end, it yielded incredible life changing results. I forgave everyone. From my mother to my family members, perpetrators, ex-boyfriends, former friends, colleagues, strangers, etc. I canceled all emotional debts that I felt were owed to me and set the captives free, only to realize that the ultimate prisoner was me. Once I went through the process of forgiving other people, I started forgiving myself and releasing all of the emotional entanglements, indictments, persecutions and convictions I had been holding against myself.

Whether we need to forgive ourselves or forgive others, refusing to forgive requires us to hold on to the blame, anger, resentment, bitterness and hatred that we feel towards them. The same is also true when we do not fully forgive ourselves. I decided to forgive so I could be free of all the emotional burdens of that were weighing me down and preventing me from living my best possible life. Forgiveness is for everyone and it doesn't matter whether we committed the offense or suffered the offense, it is over and there is nothing we or anyone else can do to change what has already happened. All we can do now is accept that it happened, learn from it and move forward. While I completely understand that some people have suffered some horrible, traumatic, life changing offenses, I know that forgiving them is not the same as condoning what they did, excusing their bad behavior, or pretending something did not happen. We can actually forgive and not reconcile or rebuild a relationship with the other person. We can also hold onto the memory without continually re-experiencing the emotion connected to the memory. To illustrate, I vividly remember giving birth to my two children and the excruciating pain of labor and delivery; however, when I think back on their births in the present, I do not re-experience the labor and delivery pains. What I now experience is the love and joy of having them in my life. It's like I have forgotten the pain.

Forgiveness may not always be an easy process, but it is a necessary one if we are to live free and prosper. Unforgiveness not only affects our mental, emotional and physical health, but it also blocks our blessings and keeps people indebted to us and us indebted to them. When I began forgiving the emotional debts owed to me, I literally had creditors cancelling financial debts I legitimately owed to them!

Letting Go

The bottom line is that forgiving and letting go frees us to live happier, healthier lives. I can honestly say that I have definitely been guilty of holding onto things including unhealthy relationships, jobs where I felt tolerated rather than appreciated, hurts and offenses from the past, and thoughts and beliefs that were outdated, self-limiting, not working and no longer serving me in the present. Because I was born eight months after the death of my father, I believe I came into the world full of fears of abandonment, loss and emptiness. As a result, the thought of losing something or someone always filled me with enormous fear and dread. I realize that part of my fear was ending up alone. So, I held on, hoping and praying the person or the thing would change on its own to protect and prevent me from having to let go and release it. I held onto painful memories because I thought that it would prevent me from further injury, betrayal and disappointment. I thought that if I released the memory or the pain, I might forget and allow it to happen again. This pattern and tendency to hold on and not let go showed up in so many areas of my life because not only did I have problems with holding on and not letting go, I also held back and couldn't let myself go. I couldn't allow things to work out for themselves and I couldn't trust anyone else to keep their word. Because we become what we think about most, these were the exact experiences that continued to show up in my life time after time. The more I began to study spiritual laws and heal my inner self, the more aware I became of the impact that holding on and holding back was not only having on my relationships, but also on my body, my peace of mind, my finances and my life as a whole. As I shared earlier, I had read countless books on the notion that our emotions are the underlying cause of physical aches, pains, conditions, abnormalities and diseases. I was already battling high cholesterol which can lead to a buildup of plaque in the arteries, seasonal allergies which cause congestion and blocked nasal passages, and indigestion which caused both irregular bowel movements and frequent constipation. Yes, when I took an honest inventory of myself, I could plainly see how holding on was causing major problems for me physically and financially. As a therapist, I would end up with financial blockages from unpaid claims and other minor issues that caused my money to be held up. I also held onto the money I had, and while I did pay all my bills on time, it was always a struggle for me due to my fear of not having enough or ending up broke. Now that I know what I know, I can pinpoint blockages in various other aspects of my life down to the point of completing this book and experiencing writer's block that kept me from writing for days or weeks!

I finally decided that holding on to toxic emotions such as anger, bitterness, resentment, self-righteousness, unforgiveness, sadness, pain and any other negative emotion was too high a cost to pay and I initiated the process of letting go. It wasn't easy, especially when a part of you believes that holding on protects you in some way or prevents things from happening to you. Because I still had those inner fears of loss and abandonment, letting go definitely came with its challenges. In fact, I am still working to completely let go of my past and all of the residual thoughts, feelings and beliefs. I am also learning to let go of the need for control in my life, and I am learning to trust and allow things to flow in me, through me and to me. I am letting go of the old outdated mental programming and conditioning along with family and societal vows, covenants and agreements. I am letting go of the need for life to be a struggle and the belief that I have to grind and wrestle for everything I get. I no longer even use the term grind and have chosen instead to say I am in flow, because I now know the power of flow and alignment as opposed to struggle and strain. I understand that struggle is a mindset that many of my ancestors had to adopt because of their situations, but one that I get to *choose* or not choose. Throughout this process, I have learned that everything in life is in constant flow and flux and when we resist by holding on, we shut down the process which causes back-ups, blockages, setbacks, congestion, and constipation. I now embrace the concept of circulation and I realize we were never meant to accumulate and hold on to anything. This really hit home for me one day when I realized the money I currently had in my wallet had been in someone else's hands the week before and someone else's hands the week before that and so on. Things are constantly in circulation and when we accept that, it will make it easier for us to let go and move on.

I have decided to let go and release anything that no longer serves me; be it physical, emotional, mental or otherwise and regardless of whether I am right, justified or did not deserve it. I simply cannot and will not pay the high cost of holding on. I am not saying we should not save money, purchase things, pay our bills, or invest; I am also not saying we cannot feel hurt or get angry at someone. What I am saying is that everything is in constant movement and our emotions were meant to be felt, expressed and released. When we forgive, release and let go, we create space for something else, something new and something better and it changes our entire lives. In the end, no one is worth our health, wealth, happiness and well-being so we must be willing to forgive and let that shit go!

Personal Reflection:

1) Write yourself a letter and forgive yourself for everything.

2) Make a list of everyone else you need to forgive, both living and deceased.

3) What are you still holding onto and how is it affecting you? (Physical issues, financial, emotional, relational)

4) How do you feel when you declutter your home, car, work space? This is the same way it feels when we detox physically and emotionally.

Chapter 12

Freedom from Guilt, Blame and Shame

"You are not what you have been through"
~~Giovanna Geathers

When we speak about forgiveness and letting go, we must also take into account the emotions we have buried and stored and three of the most toxic emotions we can experience and harbor are guilt, blame and shame. These three emotions can destroy our self-esteem, self-confidence, and self-worth, causing us to sabotage ourselves, our relationships, our health and our happiness. Earlier I shared how emotions have frequencies and the emotions of guilt, blame and shame are considered the lowest on the frequency scale, which means that when we are harboring these emotions, we are lowering our body's vibration and making ourselves susceptible to every other low-level vibration out there from car crashes to cancer. If we are going to truly live our best lives from the inside out, we will have to overcome and resolve our feelings of guilt, blame, and shame.

Guilt is defined as the feeling that we have done something wrong. Sometimes we may even feel guilty when we have been wronged if we mistakenly believed it was our fault, such as with victims of rape, sexual abuse or domestic violence. Because the person mistakenly blames and faults themselves for what has happened to them, they may feel and carry guilt for "allowing" it. Some victims have even questioned whether deep down, they may have wanted something to happen. We have all heard stories of rape victims who blamed themselves for looking or dressing a certain way, and victims of physical and sexual abuse feeling like they are somehow responsible for their experiences. Sadly, they may spend their entire lives trying to make up for their perceived wrongdoing.

Guilt imprisons us, enslaves us and often prevents us from healing and moving on from our painful experiences. Guilt can cause us to live in constant fear of being exposed and punished for our "crimes". The fear of exposure happens when we are afraid of someone finding out what we did or what was done to us. Unresolved guilt can cause us to be guarded, isolated and disconnected from people because we are inwardly afraid of someone discovering our secrets and judging us. The fear of punishment is the fear of being captured, indicted, condemned and convicted. This fear causes us to live in self-imposed prisons in our own minds. Truthfully, this fear may cause us to feel and behave no differently than criminals locked away in actual jails and prisons. If we do not forgive and set ourselves free from guilt, we can end up spending our whole lives holding back, punishing and condemning ourselves, thereby sabotaging any chance at real happiness and success; because inwardly, the guilt makes us feel as if we do not deserve it and as if we need to spend our entire existence trying to make up for our wrongs.

I once read a quote that said, "The gates of hell are locked from the inside" which means that we alone are responsible for overcoming our feelings of guilt and freeing ourselves from the mental and emotional torture it brings. If we need to confess something or make amends to someone, we must commit to doing that so we can set ourselves free. The truth is we are all deserving of forgiveness and we have the right to live free from guilt. God forgives us as far as east is from west and has promised that there is no condemnation. It is time that we learn to also forgive ourselves.

It is not enough to simply be free of guilt if we are also struggling with feelings of shame. While guilt is the feeling that we have done something wrong, shame is the belief and feeling that we ourselves are wrong. It is the difference between failing at something, and calling ourselves a "failure". Shame causes us to negatively evaluate ourselves and see ourselves as inadequate, guilty, wrong, powerless and worthless. It can occur when we fail to meet someone else's standards or expectations, but it can also occur when we fail to meet our own. Shame causes us to feel as if our whole being is flawed, defective, and wrong which in turn can lead to avoidance behaviors such as withdrawal and addiction. Shame can be deeply hidden, as the person who feels the shame often fears that someone will find out about their flaws and shortcomings. Shame is considered to be a very toxic emotion and often leads to self-rejection and self-loathing. Many times, shame is the result of painful childhood experiences such as abuse, bullying, or neglect.

According to an article in Psychology Today, children are very susceptible to taking on the shame of others who have abandoned, abused, hurt and neglected them. The child often feels as if the sole reason for the person's actions are because they - the child - are "bad". Shame is one of the main reasons many victims of sexual abuse and sexual assault will conceal what happened to them until much later in life. I have worked with several clients in their late 40's, 50's and beyond who disclosed their childhood abuse to me for the first time. Even as adults, they are still feeling responsible for what was done to them and still blaming themselves for it. These clients are usually struggling with moderate to severe depression, high anxiety, panic attacks, insomnia, and low self-esteem. As a result, they have a tendency to become involved in unhealthy and abusive relationships. Unfortunately, shame affects us at our core and causes us to question and doubt ourselves at the soul level, which is why it is so important for us to heal and be free from this heavy, toxic emotion. As long as we continue to perceive and judge ourselves as wrong, bad, defective or flawed, we will never be able to live a happy and fulfilling life and we will always struggle with self-doubt, self-rejection, self-abandonment and codependency as we learn to put other people's needs and happiness ahead of our own. Shame will cause us to have little or no boundaries in our relationships and allow people to walk all over us. It can even cause us to become abusive towards others as we project our deep-seated feelings onto them.

Lastly, blame is defined as finding fault in someone or something. The first aspect of blame I am going to explore is the blame we feel or project onto others. Blaming someone is not the same as holding them accountable and responsible for their actions. The truth is sometimes we use blame as a way of excusing our own behavior and lack of responsibility. For example, blaming a particular ethnic group or gender for our failed relationships, rather than becoming aware of and healing our own unhealthy relationship behaviors and patterns. If every man a woman dates is abusive, then at some point, she must be willing to look within herself and identify why she keeps attracting and dating the same types of men. As the saying goes, "If a dog bites you three times, it isn't the fault of the dog." Blame can and does keep us trapped in unhealthy patterns and repeating undesirable behaviors if we are unwilling to address and own our stuff. Yes, there are times when someone *is* to blame and *is* guilty of wrongdoing. The good thing is we can still hold them responsible for their actions without spending the rest of our lives playing the blame game.

Blame is another one of those toxic emotions that keeps us imprisoned and stuck if we do not process it and heal from it. We can work towards letting go of the need to blame without releasing the person from the responsibility of their actions. Likewise, we must also be willing to let go of the blame we have towards ourselves. We can own and accept responsibility for our actions, choices and behaviors without beating ourselves up and keeping ourselves imprisoned for something we said or did.

For years, I struggled with the trifecta of guilt, shame and blame without ever fully realizing or understanding the toll it was taking on my physical, mental, and emotional health; not to mention how it was causing me to hold back and sabotage myself and my relationships. When we are weighed down by guilt and shame, it will cause us to avoid true intimacy with people in our efforts to avoid exposure and possible injury. Because of my history of rape and sexual abuse, I was constantly blaming myself for what happened. I was also feeling partly to blame for my father's absence in my life and for me not being my favored by my mother. It seemed that I somehow felt responsible for every bad or negative thing that ever happened in my life. If a boyfriend broke up with me or a friend walked away, I wondered what I had done wrong, even if I knew intellectually that it wasn't about me. And because I had no real way of processing and understanding my feelings, I constantly looked for someone or something to blame for my own inner insecurities and inadequacies. I blamed my mother, I blamed my father, I blamed society, I blamed men, I blamed women and I blamed God. I had a healthy dose of blame for anyone and everyone for how and why my life was the way it was and why I had endured certain things. Even though I had always done my best to be a good person and do the right thing, deep down, the little girl in me always felt guilty, wrong, flawed, inadequate and defective. It took a lot of courage and self-reflection for me to face my past and heal from guilt, shame and blame, and there are still times when I need a reminder. Literally, during the writing of this book, I have had to coach myself several times and give myself permission to finish and drown out the negative self-talk that loves to remind me of my past mistakes, failures, shortcomings and setbacks. I am happy to say that I can now look at myself in the mirror without shame or guilt and I can forgive others and myself without hesitation or fear. As a result, I am much kinder, more compassionate and way more loving towards myself and I truly understand when the Bible talks about "setting the captives free". When we are trapped in guilt, blame and shame, we will never feel free or liberated until we face it and find the strength to heal.

Personal Reflection:

1) Are there wrongs you have suffered in life that continue to make you feel like a victim? What is this costing you?

2) Are you ready and willing to claim full responsibility for your life so you can shift from being a victim to a victor?

3) Do you struggle with the trifecta of guilt, blame and/or shame?

4) How would working through this and healing serve you?

Chapter 13

No Victims and No Villains

"There are no villains and no victims in the world"
~~Neale Donald Walsch

For much of my life, I felt like a victim. Of course, I never would have admitted it, but as I became more aware of my truth, I was able to own all of my insecurities and imperfections without judgment. Honestly, I am not even sure I knew I was playing the victim card. What I did know was that I had been through some pretty awful stuff and I felt like the world and everyone in it owed me some type of explanation, reparation or compensation for what I had endured. The truth is that I was a victim in my relationships, I was a victim in my family, I was a victim at work, I was a victim in college, I was a victim in my finances, and I was a victim even when it came to God. In short, I was the victim in my life story and there were plenty of people for me to blame. I blamed my mother, my father, my siblings, my community, my classmates, my friends, rich people, etc. Don't get me wrong, I had great reasons to justify why I was the victim and other people were to blame for it. I had grown up in a single parent home, never knowing my father, and was sexually molested and raped. I was born with what some would say were two strikes against me: I was a Black female in a small town in the south. To further my victim story, I had friends who had betrayed me, boys who broke my heart, and I lost a child due to genetic abnormalities. Yes, I was the victim in my story and sharing my story gave meaning, credibility and substance to my feelings of victimization. My story also helped me excuse and explain certain things in my life such as why I had poor boundaries in my relationships, why I was codependent on others for validation and acceptance, why I searched for love in the wrong places, and why I struggled with anger, depression and low self-esteem.

What I did not know for much of my life was that in order to play the victim, I had to continue to see myself as a victim, which meant I had to keep blaming others and making them responsible for my life. Playing the victim meant I had to keep being angry at everyone who had ever hurt me and I had to keep faulting them, resenting them and being in fear of them. It meant giving away my power and refusing to take responsibility and ownership for my own healing, happiness and well-being. Playing the victim also meant I had to have a villain and if there wasn't one, then I created one. The sad part about playing the victim is that in order to continue in that role, someone or something has to be the opposition, the adversary, the antagonist, or the enemy. This leads us to seeing life and others around us as a potential threat and because we believe the world and the people in it are a potential threat, we end up having to be extra vigilant, guarded, distrustful, and suspicious in order to prevent a possible attack. My victim story had caused me to live in fear and to believe that people and the world around me were against me. One of the things my clients who struggle with this always complain about is how exhausting it is to maintain watch and stand guard 24 hours a day, seven days a week. Maintaining this high alert status often leads to repressed anger, bitterness, resentment, depression, loneliness, isolation, anxiety, sleep disturbance, weight issues, health issues and superficial relationships that lack intimacy.

However, I do understand that many people reading this have been victimized by someone in their lives and I am in no way intending to be insensitive or undermine anyone's experience. As a therapist, I work with people every day who have been victims of rape, sexual and physical abuse, domestic violence, infidelity, racism and discrimination, sexism, neglect, rejection and abandonment, and a host of other offenses that humans seem to perpetrate against one another. I get it. I got it in my own life which is why I lived so much of it in victim mode. What I now know is that we can choose to either remain victims of our circumstances, or we can find ways to heal and overcome them. When I really began to count the cost of remaining a victim, I realized I could no longer afford it. It was then that I really started to examine what remaining a victim meant and I birthed the process of healing and transformation. I was determined to go from victim to victor. Being a victim had kept me trapped in my past, feeling hopeless, helpless, inadequate, powerless, and small. Remaining a victim made me codependent and a people-pleaser and it kept me second-guessing myself, questioning myself and always needing someone else to agree with me, affirm me, approve of me and validate me. I knew that if I was ever going to really grow, evolve and be free, I was going to have to let go of being a victim… even if I had reason. I understood that I would have to face my past, take responsibility for my healing, show up for myself and stand boldly in the present, moving intentionally and purposefully towards my future. I decided I was no longer going to be ruled by blame, shame, guilt, resentment or any other toxic emotion and I was not going to allow my past to continue to define me. I did not deny the things that had happened to me nor did I make any excuses for the people who did them. I simply decided I was no longer going to be stuck in the victim/villain cycle and just because I had been hurt, and victimized did not mean I had to remain there. I also decided I was no longer going to blame myself or feel guilty and ashamed for any of the things that I did or that were done to me. I did take responsibility for my actions and I made amends where necessary, as I embarked on the process of forgiving myself and other people. I started to understand that people were only doing the best they knew how to do, the same way I had, even though that did not justify, excuse or condone their behavior. Choosing to no longer be a victim helped me release the need to blame, criticize, condemn or hold myself and anyone else hostage. It helped me cancel their debts and free myself of the burdens of debt. Instead of remaining a victim and seeing myself as a victim of anyone or any circumstances, I decided to become the victor, the overcomer and the superhero in my story. I became 100% responsible for my life and everything in it...my joy, my peace, my happiness and my wealth, health and well-being. I also became 100% responsible for facing and overcoming my past, confronting my fears and insecurities, accepting my flaws and shortcomings, and allowing myself to be open and vulnerable. The funny thing is, when we stop being the victim in our stories, we no longer encounter as many adversaries, opponents, antagonists or villains.

The world, which I used to believe was against me, now seems to work in my favor and I meet and connect with the most incredible people who support me in my new story.

Personal Reflection:

1) Are there wrongs you have suffered in life that continue to make you feel like a victim? What is this costing you?

2) Are you ready and willing to claim full responsibility for your life so you can shift from being a victim to a victor?

3) Do you struggle with the trifecta of guilt, blame and/or shame?

4) How would working through this and healing serve you?

Chapter 14

Bounce Back

"I can be changed by what happens to me.
But I refuse to be reduced by it"
~~Maya Angelou

Resilience is defined as the ability to recover from difficulties. Another definition defines it as the power to return to your original form, position, status, etc. after being stretched, challenged, bent or compressed. Psychological resilience is the process of adapting to adversity, setbacks, trauma, tragedy and stress that may result from relationship problems, health concerns and even financial stress. In short, resilience is the ability to "bounce back" and I love to assist my clients in developing what I call their "bounce back muscles". This simply means offering them insight, feedback and tools they can utilize to better cope with whatever they are facing. Resilience is not, however, pretending you are okay when you are not, or denying your feelings to prove how strong you are; rather it is responding to life's stressors and exercising the ability to face and address it full on.

My mother was one of the most resilient people I have ever known. She went through a lot in life and I watched her go through even more prior to her transition. Actually, much of my mother's life appeared to be one crisis after another; beginning with the tragedy of my father's death that left her as a single mother raising five small children with another on the way, to working minimum wage jobs to survive and make ends meet. My mother always appeared to be in survival mode. I can remember praying that life would get easier for her and daydreaming about winning the lottery so I could buy her a big home and pay off all her bills so she would not have the stress and worry of finances anymore. On top of that, my mother had four boys, my brothers, and three of them stayed in and out of trouble. I saw my mother worry over them, fuss at them, discipline them and do everything she could to raise them to be the best men they could be with no father figure in the house. Yes, much of my life was watching and enduring my mother's constant struggles; however, all that time, I don't recall ever seeing my mother break down emotionally. I am certain things had to be difficult and weigh on her, and I am sure there were times when she wanted to give up, but all I saw was a strong, hardworking woman who was determined to get back up no matter how many times life knocked her down. My mother was the definition of resilience. Unfortunately, many people including me, also share my mother's story of being knocked down by life and having to get back up. I have now discovered that not everyone has bounce back muscles or maybe they have just never learned to use them. Resilience is what helps us heal after losing someone we love. It is what brings us back from a loss of income, our homes, cars or any other possession. It keeps us believing after we lose our status, independence, and life as we know it. It is what keeps us going after an illness, disease, accident or injury. Resilience is what helps us overcome the tragedies in life, and still turn out to be productive people. Resilience is what gets us through divorce, infidelity, and broken-heartedness. Resilience is that thing deep inside of us that won't let us say die. It is the hope that springs eternal and faith in what can and is to come. Resilience is the determination not to give up or give in and it is the willingness to get back up after we fall. Resilience is having what some would refer to as an indomitable spirit, meaning that no matter what we may have endured in life or what has come at us, no matter how hopeless things have been or appeared to be, or how much something has hurt us, we will always get back in the ring and fight another day. For me, seeing my mother fall down or get knocked down but never stay down is what taught me resilience and tenacity and what I hope to instill in my own children and my clients.

There is something in the human spirit that keeps us going, adapting, and evolving. I have read and heard of numerous people going on in the face of tremendous adversity and turning tragedy into triumph. I believe that when all is said and done, that is who we really are and what we are made of. We adapt, we survive, we get up, we bounce back and we go on. Even now in the midst of the coronavirus pandemic, we have learned to adapt to wearing face masks, maintaining social distance, figuring out ways to celebrate birthdays and say goodbye to loved ones. We have had to learn to homeschool our children and deal with business closings and job losses. This global pandemic has shown us a lot about the human spirit and our ability to bounce back after and in the midst of great tragedy. We all have a new understanding and experience of the word resilient, and I am especially grateful to my mother for teaching me early in life how to be resilient and bounce back.

Personal Reflection:

1) Do you need to increase or develop a greater sense of resilience?

2) In what areas have you already had to be resilient? How has it served you?

Chapter 15

Flow Happens

"Those who flow as life flows, know they need no other force"
~~ Lao Tzu

"Flow happens" when we are open and available. Flow is defined as movement, circulation, and passage, or the steady, continuous stream of something; flow becomes inhibited and blocked when it has no open channels or currents through which to stream. As I mentioned before, I was notorious for holding onto things, emotions, offenses and even people which certainly caused some blockages in my life.

When I was around thirty years old, I was diagnosed with high cholesterol, something that actually ran in my family. I was told I could change my diet and it would help, but because I was genetically predisposed to it, I would most likely have to take medication to manage it. I altered my diet anyway and tried several herbal supplements such as garlic, fish oil, cinnamon, and red yeast rice. I eliminated most fried foods, replaced whole milk with almond milk and cut back in other areas, but each time I went to have my blood drawn, it showed elevated levels of LDL, triglycerides and total cholesterol. As I think back to my childhood, I believe there had always been circulation issues. When I was in high school, I would get pins and needles in my legs whenever I ran. My weight lifting coach finally told me this was known as poor circulation and advised me to make sure I lubricated my skin well before each workout.

I also held onto past hurts and painful memories, thinking that if I remembered those things, I could prevent them from reoccurring. I held onto slights and offenses from people and rather than confront and address them, I buried and held back my true feelings and opinions. I even held onto happy memories out of fear that I may not have more, i.e. greeting cards, love letters, photographs and other keepsakes. In truth, I had a white knuckled grip on life and I was afraid to let go. Not letting go of things blocks flow. Not letting go blocks progress, forward movement, and the continuous stream of good in our lives. Not letting go blocks the channels and the currents for us to flow with life and allow our blessings, healing and well-being to come through.

As I became aware of the absence of flow in my finances, my health, my emotions, and my relationships, I decided then and there to eliminate and release these blockages so I could become a conduit through which life could flow. I decided to become a channel for my good and allow things to go well, for life to happen through me and for me and to be open and available for new experiences, memories and connections. I decided to create a life that was conducive to being a continuous stream of flow and movement. I was already well aware of how our thoughts, beliefs and emotions can manifest as physical conditions, ailments and diseases, so I realized I could do the work to improve my health by developing a mindset and an environment of flow.

In psychology, flow is defined as a mental state of operation in which a person performing an activity becomes fully immersed in a feeling of energized focus, involvement, and enjoyment. Star athletes, musicians, actors, and others have described flow as being "in the zone", in the pocket, in sync and a host of other colloquialisms. In metaphysics, it is called being in alignment. Regardless of the definition, the experience of it seems to be the same. Flow is what keeps us open to the experiences of life and when we release the past, we create space for something new. When we hold on and hoard, we block flow and eventually experience mental, emotional and physical constipation and congestion.

Recently during the Covid-19 pandemic, I decided to go live on Facebook with what I called "Therapy Thursdays". Each week, I covered a different topic that I thought would be relevant for people trapped inside their homes. One of the topics was *Emotional Constipation*. In this discussion, I shared all the ways that we can become emotionally constipated which is very similar to physical constipation. I received so much feedback from viewers confessing that they were constipated emotionally and could see the negative effects of it in their relationships, finances and physical bodies. One after another, people shared stories of these "blockages" in their lives from struggles with weight loss to martial conflicts and a host of other physical ailments and emotional conditions. I shared that just as we are expected to physically eliminate each day after we eat and should not go days without releasing, we should also not go days, weeks, months or years without eliminating mentally and emotionally. I now realize that we need to detox emotionally the same as we need to detox physically. When I came to this understanding, it reminded me that everything is connected from our minds to our bodies and our lives and when one area is imbalanced or blocked, it will have a significant impact in another area. I see this often with clients who release heavy emotional burdens only to also experience physical weight loss. In fact, I recently had a client who had been working out for several months with no results until she finally revealed a secret and confronted something that she had held onto for over two decades. Within a few days, she reached out to me to report that not only was she feeling emotionally lighter, she had almost instantly lost eight pounds! The truth is we must do whatever is necessary to keep our internal systems flowing the way they were designed to, so that we can keep ourselves open and clear of blocks. When we clamp down, hold tight and refuse to let go, we become reservoirs instead of channels for our good to flow to and through.

Personal Reflection:

1) Make a list and identify all areas in your life where you are experiencing blockages of any kind.

2) Identify areas where you need to let go and let things flow

3) Clean house and get rid of all mental, emotional and physical clutter of any kind.

Chapter 16

Balance & Alignment

"Only when we are in alignment with us
Soul purpose do we find true joy and inner peace"
~~Anthon St. Maarten

In this chapter, I want to talk about the concept of balance and the lessons I have learned in connection with it. For years, I have worked to create a sense of balance and harmony in my life; balance between my work life and home life, balance in my giving and receiving, and balance in my mind, body and relationships. As I previously shared, I have always been a person who has over-given, over-thought, over-analyzed, over-compensated and over-done; constantly having a need to prove myself to other people, God and the world. It is safe to say that all of this overage has caused me to be very much out of balance in many areas which has also caused me to feel out of harmony with myself and with life. When you grow up feeling inadequate, and flawed. you can develop an internal need to make up for those areas where you feel you are lacking so you can gain the approval and acceptance of others. Because of those internal feelings of lack and inadequacy, we often over-give in our relationships, overwork at our jobs, over-commit to people and activities, over-do our share, overspend, and over-compensate for every flaw, shortcoming and deficit. We may also enter and remain in unhealthy relationships to overcome, avoid or make up for those things. People who tend to overeat may be surprised to discover that they are really overcompensating for inner feelings of lack and emptiness and they eat past the point of satisfaction because they are trying to feel full. Likewise, people who tend to be long-winded when speaking are often insecure and may feel they have something to prove by overcommunicating. In reality, we have all sorts of ways of trying to make up and create a sense of balance in our lives.

I now believe that we are hard-wired to be in balance which is why an imbalance is such an issue for us and why we work so hard to fix it. Imbalances cause us to do things to try and re-establish a sense of stability which can prompt us to go above and beyond what is necessary and adequate. I also believe our true nature is that of wholeness, so it makes sense that whenever we feel like we are empty or incomplete, we will engage in behaviors to create and return to a sense of wholeness, balance and fulfillment even if those behaviors are unhealthy. Perhaps it is our mind's way of helping us maintain equilibrium. Either way, when we are feeling less than whole or out of balance in any way, we will seek out ways to re-establish it. If we feel we are not good enough, we may try extra hard to prove ourselves in order to gain external validation. If we feel unworthy, we may do things to prove our worth, even if it means overspending and going into debt so we can drive a certain car to make up for those internal feelings of worthlessness. I can tell that I have grown in this area based on a recent conversation between my son, my husband and myself where they were asking me about my dream car. I thought about it before responding that I do not have a dream car. At that moment, I realized that I have had a dream car throughout my life, but there is no vehicle that I consider my dream car at this stage. I do love driving a nice, dependable car, but I do not have a "dream car" and there is no car or truck that I need in order to feel worthy or validated. Even our bodies have a need to be in balance. We strive to balance our sleeping and waking cycles, our diets, hormones, physical activities and rest. In fact, every organ in our bodies relies on the other organs to be in balance, because an organ that does not do its share causes another organ to overwork. This is also referred to as *homeostasis* which is defined as the tendency toward a stable equilibrium between interdependent elements. This means that our bodies attempt to maintain a constant internal temperature of 98.6

degrees. A stable blood pressure and blood sugar level are two other examples of homeostasis and it is part of our body's efforts to stay balanced. When we are feeling out of balance, such as when we get cold, the body activates certain processes to bring our temperature back to a balanced state. If we become too hot, the body activates certain processes to cool us back down. Balance and the need for homeostasis and equilibrium may be one way of explaining why we tend to over-compensate in areas we feel we are lacking and inadequate. Imbalance is unnatural to us. People who are without sight often speak of how their other senses, such as hearing or touch, become extra keen and sensitive. For me, being nearsighted, I have an increased sense of hearing and smell, while my husband who does not have the best hearing has excellent eyesight. Even nature attempts to teach us the importance of balance and homeostasis through its various ecosystems which self-regulate environments for optimal living conditions despite variables such as rainfall, wind, or drought.

I believe that we were created to live in balance and harmony and the more we begin to recognize our need for balance and harmony, the more we can cease some of our over-compensating and over-doing to a more balanced state of being. When we no longer need to over-compensate, we can stop over-spending and relying on material items to bring us a sense of worth and fulfillment. We can eat better balanced meals that provide optimum nutrient absorption and maintain healthy blood sugar levels and blood pressure. We can heal from our past experiences and discover that we are indeed adequate, worthy, and good enough which will help us overcome any need to overdo anything. Some of the ways I work to maintain a sense of balance is to check in with my feelings. When I start to overdo in an area, I can usually tell because I start to feel scattered, uncentered and ungrounded. Then I commit to doing the work to bring myself back into a more balanced state of being. I am not perfect by far, but making some effort is better than nothing. Many people believe that the Covid-19 pandemic was one of the ways nature forced us all to correct some of the imbalances in the earth. I read so many stories of animals and wildlife coming out of the forests and even at my own house, we noticed squirrels playing on our front porch and a small chipmunk sitting in our window seal. We even saw an owl in our backyard for the first time living here the past fourteen years. These are things we had never witnessed before and this threat to our survival forced us to become more silent and still. Many people have shared how they became aware of the things they could live without, families started eating dinner together again and life appeared to return to simpler times. I can honestly say that since the pandemic began, I have had more rest than I have had in the past twenty years or so and I have been able to exercise more, spend more time with my husband and children and focus on what truly matters in life. I pray that we do not require another crisis like this one to remind us to slow down, rest and recharge so we can achieve and maintain some sense of balance.

Alignment

I could not write a book about wisdom and revelation without including the subject of alignment. Alignment is one of those lessons that I believe we learn over and over again, perhaps because for whatever reason we tend to forget the importance and relevance of it. I, for sure, was out of alignment and had been for many years. Even though, I was unaware of the root causes of being out of alignment, I certainly was aware of the effects. It was during my epiphany season that I began to understand the true impact of being out of alignment and the essential need for balance and recalibration.

Alignment essentially means being in proper position. For example, when a car is out of alignment, we can usually tell by the way it drives. The car will tend to veer to one side of the road and will be hard to straighten. We may have uneven tread wear, a crooked steering wheel even when we're driving straight, and squealing tires.

When a car is in alignment, it drives straight, is easy to maneuver, and we can actually remove our hands from the steering wheel and the car will continue to travel in a straight line on its own for a period of time. When a home appliance is out of alignment, it does not perform or function properly, such as an a/c unit needing coolant. Without the necessary repairs or adjustments to bring it back into alignment, it will not perform as expected.

Just like our vehicles, appliances, and many other material things in our lives benefit from being in alignment, our bodies, minds, emotions and spirits also need to be in alignment. Thankfully for us, they too will let us know when we are out of line or misaligned. We can tell that our bodies are out of alignment when we experience fatigue, indigestion, insomnia or excessive sleepiness, constipation or diarrhea, loss of appetite or increased appetite, unexplained weight loss or weight gain, headaches, inflammation, aches and pains or more serious symptoms of disease. When we are mentally out of alignment, we may have difficulty concentrating and we may experience brain fog, mental confusion, poor memory recall, racing thoughts, recurring nightmares or disturbing dreams, or more serious mental health conditions. Emotional misalignment can be characterized by feelings of sadness, depression, anxiety, panic, overwhelm, hopelessness, helplessness, irritability, and mood swings. Contrary to popular misbelief, all mood swings are not an indication of a mental disorder and may simply be a symptom of misalignment, such as hormonal imbalances, grief, trauma or other major life changes.

Being out of spiritual alignment can be defined as not knowing who we are at the core of our being which may cause us to constantly seek external validation, approval, and acceptance. Instead of trusting and knowing that everything we seek is already within, we instead look to other people, relationships, things, and accomplishments to find meaning, purpose and a sense of fulfillment. Being out of spiritual alignment could also mean not being aligned with our higher source of intelligence and power, and not believing or trusting that there is something bigger than ourselves.

It is safe to say that I was probably out of alignment in every area of my life and I had the evidence to show for it. The Bible says that "you shall know a tree by the fruit it bears" and if we are inwardly out of alignment, it will definitely show up on the outside, no matter how much we try to hide and conceal it. My misalignment was showing up in my friendships, relationships, health, and also in my body, emotions, thoughts, worship and even my finances and slowly, but surely revealing my fruits.

Perhaps the spiritual misalignment was the worst because years earlier, I had abandoned my relationship with God. I don't mean this in a religious sense, but I mean the close, intimate relationship I had with God even before I knew what to call Him. When I was a child, I used to sit and just feel the presence of God around me. I wasn't afraid of it nor did I need to rationalize it. I knew enough to know it wasn't an imaginary friend and my inner knowing told me that it was something bigger than me, deeper than me, and yet closely connected to me and never out of reach. I not only felt connected and attached to it, I felt aligned with it. Then when I discovered the betrayal of my ex-boyfriend and made my "Declaration of Independence", I disconnected and severed my close relationship with God. What's crazy about this is that despite all the other painful experiences in my life, I had never questioned my faith until then. The hurt, anger and disappointment I felt caused me to withdraw, detach and ultimately retreat. To say I was out of spiritual alignment is an understatement. I was a spiritual train wreck and I spent the next several years running, ducking, dodging, avoiding, questioning and self-destructing as a result of my misalignment. When I did make attempts to reconnect spiritually, it was always fleeting and easily shaken. I would go to church, or have a spiritual experience at home or work and feel that connectedness once again, but within hours, days, or weeks. I would be right back in that same empty place. Despite my best efforts to reconnect and realign myself with God, there was a part of me that remained disconnected and out of alignment. When I began to fully understand the importance and necessity of being in alignment and what had led to my being out of alignment, I was able to see why I could never recapture that original feeling, when I could feel God's presence with me and within me without effort and I had this inner certainty and didn't need anyone to confirm or validate it. It was a connection that was almost magical and it had been missing for years. The reality of it was that I had not fallen out of alignment and I had not "lost" my connection or my faith. I had willingly abandoned it and just like the story of the prodigal son in the Bible, God had always been right there waiting with open, loving arms. The gate had never been locked and I had always had access to enter. Discovering this truth made such a difference to me and it re-opened my eyes of understanding to so many things, giving me the reassurance that if I am the one who walked away and abandoned my faith, then I am also the one capable of reclaiming, reconnecting and realigning. I truly believe that in order for us to live an enriching and fulfilling life, it is essential that we strive towards maintaining a sense of spiritual, mental, physical and emotional alignment. While we may not be able to do this 100% because life happens, we can always keep making those adjustments until everything is fully aligned again.

Just as it is necessary for us to be aligned within ourselves, we must also be in alignment with our desires. If we desire good things, good relationships, good health, wealth and vitality, we must be alignment with those things or else we cannot attract them into our lives. It is similar to a radio station frequency. No matter how much you want to hear a certain station, you must be tuned into the right frequency to pick up that station. The same is true for us when it comes to manifesting the things we desire. Being in alignment with what we desire is the fastest way for us to bring about the manifestation of it. Otherwise you will continue to experience the same frustration and disappointment from working hard and seeing little or no results.

I am still working to create alignment in all areas of my life and I can only imagine this will be a lifelong process because there are always things that can and do throw us out of alignment, just as a car gets thrown out of alignment if it hits a large pothole. If we do find ourselves out of alignment, we can simply recalibrate ourselves until we are back in balance.

Personal Reflection:

1) Are you out of balance? How is this affecting you?

2) Are there areas of your life that are out of physical, emotional, mental or spiritual alignment?

3) What are some ways you can begin the process of recalibration?

Chapter 17

Rest and Relaxation

"You don't always need to be getting stuff done.
Sometimes it's perfectly okay, and absolutely necessary,
to shut down, kick back, and do nothing"
~~Lori Deschene

In the Fall of 2018, I learned for the first time the true meaning of rest. Not rest as in sleep, but rest while I was awake and alert. I had been working a lot and was feeling very tired, overwhelmed and out of balance. Let me say that I love what I do and I love it so much that it is sometimes hard for me to stop. During this time, I was sleeping pretty well at night, but there were still times when I would awaken early to think something through. I remember telling a friend that I hardly ever felt like I was "off", but at the time I was referring to being a mother of two young children and a wife. I worked five days a week and spent weekends at sporting activities, birthday parties or attending some other family function. After a suggestion from my sister to only work four days per week, I stopped working on Tuesdays and finally, I had a day off to myself to sleep in, sit in silence and do whatever I wanted to do. Most weeks I did not even turn on the TV or the radio. It felt good, it felt relaxing and it was rejuvenating. Because of my day off, I would go back to work the next day feeling somewhat revived, but I still felt tired, anxious, unbalanced and stressed. One particular day as I was feeling unusually stressed and anxious, I began praying and meditating. Because I was already on my journey towards healing and wholeness, I remained open to whatever revelations and epiphanies life would offer me. I thought of all the responsibilities I had as a business owner, wife, mother, sister, aunt, and friend, and I thought of how, as much as I loved the people and the conditions in my life, I was working really hard to keep all my balls in the air. Truth be told, I was constantly striving to be a great wife and an even better mother. I was working hard to be a great therapist and continue to expand my thriving practice. I was working hard to create financial wealth for our family. Despite all my noble intentions, the reality was that I was exhausted, I was drained and I was spent. It was then that I began to seek wisdom and understanding. What came to me was that I had mastered the art of working hard and I had mastered the art of trying to do it all myself. What I had not mastered was how to let go, trust the process and rest. During this time, I felt as if God personally sat me down, held out His massive hands and told me to cast all my cares upon Him. I literally began to cry as I realized I did not even know how to rest without feeling guilty about it. I remember feeling guilty for taking a nap because I always felt like I should have been up doing something. I slowly realized that the only time I truly allowed myself to rest, other than being asleep at night, was when I was sick. Then, somehow, I felt it was okay for me to rest and do nothing because it would be excused, but even then, I only allowed myself a few days to be down and then it was time to get back in the game. When I prayed and asked God where this had come from, He reminded me of my constant need to prove myself. He was right. All of my life, I had been constantly working to prove my worth, my value, and even to justify my existence on the planet. I felt like I always had to prove that I was capable, competent and qualified. Even more so, I had to prove I could do it alone. The truth was I did not know how to ask for help and even when I did, I felt guilty, undeserving, inadequate and weak. I was carrying such heavy burdens of responsibility and obligation that it was no wonder I started to experience heart palpitations and anxiety. God then began to reveal to me the meaning of rest. First, He showed me an image of myself swimming upstream against the current while others were floating effortlessly downstream. Initially, this bothered me because the perfectionist part of me saw this as laziness and shiftlessness which I could never allow myself to be; but as I became willing to relax my old way of thinking, I slowly understood that this was simply a mindset I had that told me life could not just flow and be easy. This mindset told me that life is hard and hard work is the only way to be successful. While I still believe hard work is essential to success, I now know that we have a choice in how we see life and we can choose to flow with life, floating effortlessly downstream, trusting God and the process, or we can choose to continuously work against life, doing it ourselves, struggling and swimming upstream. When I realized I had been swimming upstream against the current of life in my efforts to prove myself, and I saw that I could begin to allow things to happen for me rather than me having to force open every door and fight every battle alone, I truly started to understand the meaning of rest. Rest is not just resting *from* our work, but resting *in* our work. It is when we do our part, but then we let go and trust God and the universe to do its part. Rest is when we cast our cares upon God and release our burdens of worry and fear. Rest is when we trust that everything happens for our good in the end. Yes, there may be times when we have to persevere or keep at it, but even in those times, we can decide to be at rest in our minds and in our bodies. Rest is a mindset and it relies heavily on our ability to trust...trust ourselves, trust life, trust God and trust the process. Finally, I understood that I had nothing to prove and I understood that I was already qualified, competent, adequate and good enough. I understood that life was not my enemy and the universe really was for me. I understood that somehow things would work out for me and I could lean on God and trust Him to do what is best, because He loves and cares for me.

Just Breathe

Several years ago, when I decided to launch "Breathe", I had no idea it would evolve into a brand and a movement. Initially, I got the idea from someone who invited me to a breathing session. Then,

I began to research and study the concept of the breath and breath work. I read the book, *Breathe*, by Dr. Belisa Vranich and I studied the different types of breathing techniques such as the Oshun breath, prana, 4:7:8 breathing and many others. Slowly, I began to introduce deep breathing into my counseling sessions, especially with people who were struggling with anxiety, stress and panic attacks, and I was amazed at the effects of this simple yet effective tool that cost nothing and was readily available anytime. I discovered that breathing is one of only two bodily functions that is both conscious and automatic (blinking is the other one) and how significantly it could shift someone's mood. I saw clients who came in highly agitated leave in a state of complete calm and relaxation. I would ask them to give an SUD (subjective unit of distress) rating at the beginning and at the end. The first number would often be at least a six or higher and after the breathing session, it would always be a one or two. Perhaps the most amazing transformation happened with an actively suicidal client. I was literally on the verge of calling 911 to have this client hospitalized when something inside of me said "Breathe". I lead her through about ten to fifteen minutes of conscious, deep breathing and the shift was almost unbelievable. Even she was in awe and asked if she could use this on her own. Absolutely, I replied. I then began recommending it as an at-home treatment for all of my clients to address stress, panic, overwhelm, anxiety and trauma. I had read about how trauma causes us to breathe from the chest area rather than from the diaphragm, and I have witnessed firsthand how many of my clients look as if they are holding their breath and how people who have been wounded by life are almost afraid to relax and breathe deeply for fear of letting down their guards and being reinjured again. These clients are in a constant state of fight, flight or freeze. They are hyper-aroused, hardly ever at rest and their shallow breathing is one of the most noticeable indications of this. I became intentional about deep breathing and I launched breathing sessions in my office. People who were not even clients attended and loved them. I was once asked to do a seminar on Compassion Fatigue for the local Department of Social Services and at the end of my presentation, I lead a group of social service workers in a five-minute breathing exercise. From my position on stage, I could visibly see the looks of amazement on people's faces and afterwards several of them approached me saying they had not felt that calm and relaxed in a long time. I have even seen people shed tears during breathing sessions. After that, I knew that I was onto something. People needed to breathe. I needed to breathe. And not just unconsciously, but consciously and intentionally, and not just clients who were struggling with panic and anxiety, but anyone needing to reduce stress and get better at coping with life and its many challenges and demands.

We now live in a time where people are more stressed than ever, and with stress being one of the major underlying factors of disease or dis-ease, it is essential that we learn to relax, be still and breathe. After witnessing the effects of deep breathing with clients, laypeople and social service workers, I launched The Breathe Shoppe and began offering aromatherapy products and other inspirational items designed to help people breathe better physically, emotionally and spiritually. From there, I founded The Breathe Group on Facebook and engaged in sharing inspirational insights and exercises with the members. In 2017, I held the first Breathe Retreat for Women at a mountain retreat center forty minutes outside of town and 32 women, the majority African-American, attended and were greatly impacted. It was a full day of breathing, yoga, and other mindfulness exercises and techniques. The following year, I hosted the second Breathe Retreat and again it sold out, and again it was 99% African-American women. What I also noticed was how much Black women seemed to need this and I discovered that many of us suffer from what I call The Superwoman Syndrome. I even wrote a whole chapter on this in my first book, and I have facilitated workshops around it and discussed it on my radio show. The, women of all races began reaching out and sharing with me how overwhelmed, stressed out and depressed they were. Because of the Superwoman Syndrome, women often do not allow themselves to practice self-care or reduce their level of responsibility out of fear of appearing weak or incompetent. At my events, I encourage women to give themselves permission to de-stress and take better care of themselves. I stress that self-care is not a luxury, it is a necessity for our mental, emotional and physical health. I educate women on the link between stress and being overweight as well as stress and disease, and I share how our constant state of doing, robs us of our happiness and well-being. After the second successful Breathe Retreat, I held the first Breathe Women's Conference in my hometown of Greenville, SC and brought in speakers from Atlanta, Charlotte, and throughout SC for a full day of empowerment, mindfulness and inspiration. I reiterated to the women that it is okay to relax, live and breathe. In 2019, I took the Breathe Retreat to Arizona and a group of women from SC accompanied me to Phoenix for a phenomenal three-day getaway in the desert. Again, I saw women being transformed before my eyes through the power of focused relaxation, self-care and deep inner healing work.

Shortly after the second Breathe Women's Conference, I became more aware of the breath from a spiritual perspective, although I already knew there was a direct connection. During my breathing sessions, I would always remind the participants that "breathing is the first thing we do when we are born and the last thing we do when we die". I also knew there were several references in the Bible about the Breath of God and the breath of life, but I had not really grasped how powerful the connection was until I discovered the concepts of *ruah* and *pneuma*. *Ruah* or *ruach*, a Hebrew word, and *pneuma* which is Greek both mean wind or breath and are also translated as "Spirit". Not only do I now have an understanding of the breath in a physical and emotional capacity, but I realize that our breath is the Spirit of God alive on the inside of us. It is literally what keeps us alive and when we die, it is said that we have taken our last breath.

Even though much of my focus with the Breathe movement has been on women, I have also discovered that men too have a need to breathe and practice self-care. Recently, The Breathe Group began hiking in nearby areas around town. On one of our trips, a male paramour of one of the women came along and observed us but did not participate. The following week, I received a message from him stating he had witnessed how powerful our hike and breathing session was and felt like men needed to have those same experiences. More men began reaching out to me about the need for self-care and I was asked to begin leading men's conferences to assist men in their healing. Even though, I have always worked with men individually or in couples' therapy, I am now seeing a surge of men desiring to become more mentally and emotionally healthy.

The power of the breath is truly transformative and the beauty of it is that our breath is always with us. While it is true that we are breathing anyway each day, conscious breathing is an essential way of managing stress, anxiety, and distress in our lives. It costs us nothing other than the time and commitment to do it. I have had clients share testimonies of how their breath work has reduced test anxiety, performance anxiety in sports or on stage and even helped them refrain from emotionally reacting with their partners, greatly reducing the frequency of arguments and conflict. I encourage you to research the many other benefits of deep breathing such as lowered blood pressure, pain relief, increased energy, better sleep, toxin removal and an improved immune and digestive system. I also encourage you to develop a practice of regular self-care and make it a part of your life instead of a random feel-good experience. You may be surprised at how much calmer, happier, and more at peace you begin to feel.

Personal Reflection:

1) Do you feel rested?

2) How can learning to rest benefit you?

3) How do you practice self-care?

4) How can you begin a regular practice of deep breathing and relaxation?

5) How might you benefit from being calmer and more at ease?

Chapter 18

Being Unbothered

"Me. Unbothered. Moisturized,
In my lane, Well-hydrated, Flourishing"
~~Cardi B

If you had asked me a few years ago or even a few months ago if I would be writing a chapter on being unbothered, I would have laughed right in your face! I have lived a life of being bothered! Bothered by things, bothered by the weather, bothered by other people, and bothered by situations. The truth of the matter is that I was guarded, defensive and "bothered". Being bothered means to be agitated, annoyed, pestered, worried or troubled. I grew up with a brother who seemed to exist for the sole purpose of bothering me, pestering me, and annoying me with some new prank or act of mischief. Looking back on it now, it was all harmless fun, but it sure did not feel that way at the time. And it seemed the more bothered I was, the more he bothered me. I can laugh about it now, but I can recall being constantly teased and picked on because he knew eventually it would get to me and I would react in some emotional way. I would get angry and yell at him to leave me alone which only added fuel to the fire and encouraged him to continue. Many times, it ended with me sulking in my room close to tears because I felt powerless and frustrated to stop him from bothering me. I took it all so personally and any bait he threw out would snag me hook, line, and sinker.

Years later as an adult, I still allowed things and people to bother me, such as people not liking me or supporting me and people speaking negatively about me or wrongfully accusing me of something. I became bothered by friendships ending and things not going my way. At the time, I did not know how those things were really affecting me and I did not understand that allowing those things to trigger me was causing unnecessary worry and stress in my mind and body. Not only did it have the power to dampen my mood, it could ruin my whole day. I was constantly reacting to other people's comments, slights, rejections, and objections and I did not understand then that I was giving all my power away to things, people and circumstances. Ultimately, I realized I was allowing them to run my life. I had not yet learned how to manage my energy and I was unfamiliar with the freedom of being "unbothered". What I also realize is how maintaining a state of being easily bothered seemed to attract more things into my life to bother me, such as slow drivers to new cashiers and everything in between.

My freedom came while riding to my women's brunch with my best friend from Arizona. We were discussing some things we had encountered on our journeys and she made a statement that "Even though some things bother her, she is unbothered". Wow! That hit me like a ton of bricks as I said to myself, "You mean you can have things that bother and annoy you and yet still remain unbothered?" After that day, I began to take serious inventory of all the things that I had allowed to bother me over the years, things that when I really thought about them meant nothing in the grand scheme of things. I knew firsthand the effects of stress on our minds, emotions and bodies and I understood that becoming unbothered would mean a drastic reduction in my stress levels. I came to realize that not everything or everyone deserved or necessitated a response from me. I also learned to identify my emotional triggers and that I could respond to things and situations rather than automatically react to them. I learned that I have the power to choose what moves me and I reminded myself I am not a victim. I also discovered that being unbothered did not mean being callous or uncaring, but rather being unmoved and unaffected by everyone and everything around you.

Being unbothered means choosing to live in peace with the knowledge of who we really are without the approval and validation of others. It means keeping my word to myself, saying what I mean and meaning what I say, staying in my lane and minding my own business first. It means choosing not to worry and trusting God to handle things in my best interest. It means knowing I am not required to save the world and fix everyone and everything in it. It means knowing I am enough and that what I have is enough and what I give is enough. It means setting limits and boundaries with myself and with others. It means prioritizing myself and making self-care a regular practice and not a once in a while treat. It means letting go and forgiving without hesitation, no matter the offense and it means no longer carrying the baggage from my past, which I cannot change anyway. It means trusting myself and trusting the process.

Let me say that I am still a work in progress and I continue to identify what triggers me and make the conscious choice of whether or not I should respond. Honestly, most times, I realize a response is not needed and I smile as I feel that sense of peace inside. When I do need to respond, I try to calm myself down first before responding so I can choose my words and reactions wisely instead of reacting emotionally. I don't always get it right and I am perfectly okay with that. I can honestly tell you I feel more in control and more powerful now that I know it is my choice to be bothered or unbothered and that I can do the work to heal from my emotional triggers. We all have things that bother us and we all have emotional triggers, but like me, you no longer have to be a victim of your emotions and you can choose your response. When you do, you take back your power and you discover more happiness, joy, and peace.

Personal Reflection:

1) What triggers you?

2) How can knowing your triggers help you in not reacting?

3) How can becoming unbothered benefit you?

Chapter 19

Happiness

"Clap along if you feel like a room without a roof"
~~Pharrell

I can vividly remember when the song, *Happy*, was released by recording artist, Pharrell. Just listening to it lifted my spirits and improved my mood on countless occasions. It has even moved me to dance and clap whenever I heard it. I mean, don't we all just want to be happy? As a therapist, "being happy" is the number one goal my clients share with me when discussing their treatment expectations whether in individual, family or couple's therapy. If happiness is what we all seem to be seeking, then why is it that so many of us find it to be missing and elusive? To date, there are thousands of books on the subject of happiness and thousands of life coaching programs, seminars, Ted Talks, workshops, e-courses, hypnosis and subliminal programs - all designed to help us find and maintain happiness. In our search for happy, we often try many things to elicit and create this desirable feeling. We purchase things, travel, eat, enter into relationships, take up new hobbies, go to college, and choose or change careers in our never-ending search for happiness. Yet despite an unlimited amount of freedom in America, unrestricted access to the internet and the ability to own every gadget and invention known to man, we are unhappier than we have ever been. It is a known fact that rates of depression and suicide have continued to rise each year among children, adolescents and adults. People of various ages, races and genders are regularly seeking treatment for depression or using other methods of self-medication in their efforts to avoid, alleviate or at least dampen their feelings of unhappiness and unfulfillment.

While I do not profess to have discovered the secret to happiness, I do intend to share my insight and understanding on the subject from my own personal experiences and discoveries along with some of my professional encounters with clients. I also do not wish to imply that depression is simply a feeling of unhappiness, because as a clinician, I understand that depression can stem from a variety of underlying issues and manifest as a plethora of different symptoms, unhappiness being only one of them. Additionally, it is quite possible to feel unhappy and not be depressed. So, what is happiness and why is it so hard to find?

When I was a child, I believed that in order to be happy, you had to have certain things. I believed that you had to be rich to be happy, live in the right neighborhood, own a business or live in a big house with central air conditioning. I believed happiness came from earning a degree or an advanced degree and getting the right job in your chosen field. Happiness for me was also about having a great wardrobe, being the right body size and shape, owning the latest gadget, having lots of friends, traveling, and marrying the perfect person. None of what I believed, heard, saw or experienced ever suggested to me that happiness was an inside job and that it was not contingent or dependent on external conditions or the presence or absence of any person, place or thing. That…I would learn the hard way.

In 2004, I began what I now refer to as my dark night of the soul when I started experiencing frequent bouts of anxiety that seemed to come from out of nowhere. At the time, I had finished graduate school, and while I wasn't working in the counseling field for which I was educated and trained, I had landed a pretty decent job as Director of a nonprofit program that served children and older adults in a low-income community. I had also moved back home with my mother to save money, pay off bills and improve my credit so I could buy my first home. In fact, I even completed a real estate course and started investing in real estate. In 2005, I purchased my first investment property and turned it into a rental property. I then later bought land from my mother upon which I built my first new construction home and sold it to my sister. I was making a lot of money and to celebrate, I bought my first fully equipped luxury car. From the outside looking in, I had all the trappings of success and happiness. I was in my early 30's, attractive, healthy, in great shape and having a wonderful time enjoying life with my friends and family; however, in spite of all this, I still found myself experiencing periods of fear, panic, sadness and anxiety that eventually turned into mild to moderate depression. It was frustrating and I could not figure out what was missing, because outwardly I seemed to have it all. I also could not identify why I continued to feel a sense of emptiness inside. I had material things, I had relationships with people, I had a place to live and a career, yet I was experiencing a mixture of sadness, unfulfillment, loneliness, and unhappiness. At that time, I was still unfamiliar with how feelings that have been buried inside can come back to haunt you, despite outside appearances. I was still new to the counseling profession and I was too proud to actually seek the services of a qualified therapist. Instead, I sought out and tried every holistic, natural alternative I could find. I saw a naturopathic doctor, I had blood work done to assess my hormone levels, I fasted, I meditated, I recited curse breaking prayers, I went to church, and I praised and pleaded to God for relief. Once, I even traveled two hours to see a deliverance minister and have her lay hands on me, and I anointed myself with holy water I obtained from the local Catholic church. I started researching the emerging field of energy medicine and energy therapy healing techniques such as EFT (Emotional Freedom Technique). I tried aromatherapy and all sorts of natural supplements including St. John's Wort, Sam-E, 5-HTP, Bach Rescue Remedy and other homeopathic blends. I was drowning in despair and desperation and yet I did not want anyone else to know what I was experiencing. I had bought into the concept that strong people, especially resilient African-American women like me, did not get depressed or experience anxiety. And even though I was trained as a psychotherapist, I also knew the stigma around mental health in my culture and therefore dismissed the notion of seeking professional help.

After celebrating my 35th birthday and having struggled with these feelings for two years, I decided that maybe my anxiety and depression were related to abandonment issues associated with the absence of my father. I was already familiar with the impact that daddy issues can have on our self-esteem and self-worth, so I finally mustered up enough courage to reach out to my mother and visit my father's grave. I was shocked and slightly embarrassed to learn that he was buried not more than twenty minutes from where I had grown up and spent most of my life, and I had never been to his grave. The following week, I asked my mother and my father's sister, to accompany me to the cemetery where my father was "resting in peace". As I stood at the foot of my father's grave, I prayed that this would help heal some of my broken-heartedness. Standing there in the rain that day, I began to feel a glimmer of hope as some of the missing pieces of my life started falling into place. However, my issues were far from over and it would be at least ten more years before I would intentionally start to face and address my past issues.

In 2007, I met and became involved in a new relationship with a man who is now my husband. At the time, we were expecting the birth of our first child. Not only was I ecstatic about becoming a mother, but for the first time in a long time, I was involved with someone who was good for me and to me. Yet, despite all of these factors, I continued to feel broken, incomplete and unhappy on the inside. Frustrated, I decided then and there that I would no longer live in that space of darkness and unfulfillment. I decided that I was tired of hiding and pretending everything was okay and that no matter what my culture or society had to say, I was worthy and deserving of true happiness. With much trepidation, I reached out to a therapist and began the process of doing my own inner healing work. It took me three full years of searching, purging, releasing, restoring, reclaiming and reconciling to heal from the damage that I had suffered throughout my life. I could no longer run and hide and deny anything I was experiencing, and it was through this process that I began to really know myself, like myself and accept myself. It was then that I realized what happiness was.

As I shared earlier, with the release of my first book on love and relationships, I revealed to the world my personal story of rejection, abandonment, rape, sexual abuse, low self-esteem, low self-worth, and poor self-image. I shared my journey of being in unhealthy relationships searching for external validation, approval and acceptance. I bore my soul for everyone to see and surprisingly discovered that instead of feeling exposed, ashamed and embarrassed by my vulnerability, I felt liberated, powerful and unencumbered for the first time! What was even more incredible was the number of people who were inspired by my story and liberated from their own shame and embarrassment. It was then that I stopped searching outside of me, looking to others for my happiness and fulfillment, and truly began to seek it within my own self. It was then that I discovered I would never find it in my relationships, my social status, my bank account or my personal and professional achievements. I would not find it in superficial things such as my body size or my material possessions. I realized and accepted that I was responsible for creating and maintaining my own happiness and it had to come from the inside. Otherwise, it would always fluctuate depending on what was going on in my life at a particular time. I discovered that my happiness and my joy were not just reactions to good news or accomplishing a goal, but my happiness is a state of being that I get to nurture and cultivate within. It was that discovery that enabled me to stop chasing and searching for happiness and just "BE" happy. Once I realized that I had the power to choose my reactions and responses to things, my happiness became a choice that I consciously chose to make despite what was going on in and around me.

Like the majority of people, I had always believed that happiness was a feeling or a set of circumstances and conditions. Mistakenly, we think "I'll be happy when, if and eventually", when the best time for us to be happy is right now, in this very moment. The state of happiness is understanding the difference between being happy "about" or "with" a particular thing as opposed to being happy in spite of it. For example, we may not be happy about losing a job or our marriage ending, but we can still choose to be happy in the midst of those circumstances even if we are not happy about said circumstances. We may not be happy with certain challenges we have to face, but we can choose to be happy within ourselves as we face those challenges. I am not suggesting for us to be happy with the death of a loved one or any other life altering experience because as humans, we are meant to experience a wide range of emotions and sadness. grief, shock, and anger are normal emotional reactions in certain situations. However, I want us to remember that our emotions are temporary and can fluctuate from day to day or even within the same day. Have you ever awakened in a great mood and then received disturbing news that caused you to feel anxious and irritated by the evening? Likewise, have you ever woken up feeling down and hopeless and ended up having an incredible day?!

Happiness is a state of mind, an attitude and a choice, unless you are one of those very lucky people who is just happy and upbeat naturally. I am not. Perhaps due to the trauma surrounding my dad and my birth or maybe other life experiences that have deeply affected my emotions, I have to consciously choose to remain happy, joyful and grateful even when I am going through challenges and setbacks or am not "feeling" happy. I get to choose to focus on what I am grateful for and what is working in my life as a reminder to myself of what is still possible. Is this always easy for me? No, but it is always doable.

As I complete this chapter on happiness, our country and our world are in the midst of the Covid-19 pandemic. Many businesses have shut down, schools have closed and people are quarantined within their homes and communities. While I certainly am not happy we are in this current state of crisis or that people are dying or losing their jobs, I am happy that we live in a time when we have access to things such as e-learning so we can continue to educate our children, as well as technology and internet that allow us to work from home and still connect with people on social media and other platforms. While there are many emotional reactions I could choose from such as anger, fear, worry, and panic, I know that none of those will cause this situation to be resolved any faster; therefore, I choose to pray for those who have been negatively affected and work to keep my own thoughts and energy positive, so that I do not add to the level of misery and suffering.

In conclusion, I believe that happiness is our birthright and happiness is our natural state of being. I believe that due to circumstances and experiences, we forget this and begin searching for something on the outside that we already have an unlimited access to inside. We will not find happiness "out there, in them, or in that". Money will not guarantee us happiness nor will success or achievement. I have seen this regardless of if I am working with very wealthy clients or those of limited means. All have experienced the frustration of looking for happiness outside of themselves. It's also true that if happiness was not our natural state, then it wouldn't bother us so much to be unhappy.

I know for some people; this may sound or feel impossible and unattainable. Maybe you feel you have tried everything and nothing has worked. Maybe you have given up and decided it is just not for you. The reality is that you will be required to do the work to heal, as I did, from the things that continue to haunt you and distort your perceptions of the truth. Do not try to trick yourself into happiness with the accumulation of things, do not try to fake happiness and pretend to feel something you do not, and do not try to force your partner to be responsible for your happiness or take on the responsibility for their happiness. Instead, be willing to face yourself, deal with your stuff and be happy and fulfilled from the inside out.

Personal Reflection:

1) Do you know what makes you happy? Sometimes it's simple things such as watching the sun rise or walking on the beach at twilight.

2) If happiness is inside, how can you begin to recognize and make the choice to be happy, no matter what you may be experiencing? Remember you may not be happy *about* the situation, but you can be happy *within* the situation.

3) When you accept that happiness is an inside job, how does this make you feel?

4) How can you embrace your happiness now?

Chapter 20

Abundance & Awareness

"Abundance is not something we acquire,
it is something we tune into"
~~Dr. Wayne Dyer

I can still recall the day that I received a life changing revelation about the quote from Dr. Dyer that "Abundance is not something we acquire, it is something we tune into", but first, let me share some of the backstory.

A few months after my husband and I were married in 2012, we discussed and decided that I would quit my job of nine years and open my own private psychotherapy practice. In preparation for this, I paid off all of my expenses other than my monthly occurring bills in order to lessen the weight of having only one income. On top of that, we found out I was pregnant with our daughter and my husband's insurance had a much higher deductible than I had at my previous job. In addition, my husband was commuting over an hour each way to his job in another city and gas prices were unusually high during that time. So, there we were with only one stable income, a gas bill of over $700 a month and we were still paying off bills from our wedding. We were also paying private Catholic school tuition for our son and infant care for our daughter. The stress and strain of that first three years of our marriage was almost unbearable, but instead of it causing us to argue, it brought us closer together. Because things were so tight financially, I began praying and seeking insight on how to increase our monthly income and get us out of our financial bind. I was already faithfully paying tithes and because I was familiar with the Law of Attraction, I was using every method and technique I knew of to bring in more money. My church had a practice of having us name our seed on the tithe envelope and for months, I wrote down "Increase in finances". One day, as I was about to write that down again, I heard God say, "Don't ask for more money, ask for an abundant mindset". At the time, I was unsure what that meant, but I thought to myself, "I'll try it and see what happens". A few weeks later, I received another revelation from God that said "If you get an increase in money and you still have a poverty mindset, then you won't be able to manage it or maintain it and you will end up right back in the same place". If we do not raise our financial setpoint or increase our capacity to receive, we end up back in the same position as we started. I then reflected on the times I had heard of lottery winners losing all their winnings within a short time and ending up being worse off than they were before. I began studying up on how to develop an abundant mindset. A short time after that, I stumbled on the quote by Dr. Wayne Dyer about abundance and I instantly knew this was in response to my dilemma, so I decided to meditate on it and see what insights I received so I could grasp the full meaning of it. I thought about my current definition of abundance which was most certainly focused on the acquisition of money and material items such as cars, homes, clothes, and jewelry and all the other things you could buy with money. What did it mean though to tune into abundance? One thing I now live by is that when you ask a question and you remain open to discovery, you will most certainly receive an answer. The day I finally experienced an aha moment and received the epiphany on tuning into abundance changed my life! What I immediately understood was that "everything I desire already exists and the only reason I am not aware of it is because I am tuned in to the absence of it rather than the presence of it". I was then led to meditate on and "tune in" to all the money I currently had in my life in the form of cash, coins, checks, deposits, etc. When I finished, I had listed about seventeen current areas of money from my bank accounts down to the coins in the cupholder of the car. The amount of money was irrelevant as I realized with astonishment that money was indeed all around me. God then encouraged me to meditate on all of the intangible forms of money; books I could sell, products in my retail shop, office furniture not being used, as well as clothes and shoes I was no longer wearing. This list became even more robust as I thought about business ideas not yet birthed, books not yet written, products not yet developed and so on. I began to feel an inner excitement at the realization that abundance was all around me in both tangible and intangible forms and I was completely unaware of it because I had never tuned into it. I then thought of all the new construction going on in my hometown, new cars being sold and driven, and new businesses being launched, all of which are evidence of abundance. I soon discovered that abundance was everywhere and I simply had to tune in and become aware of it. I was already familiar with the power and the magic of practicing gratitude, so I gave thanks for an abundance of time, health, love, friendship and yes even money. I gave thanks for an abundance of clients, customers, participants, resources and ideas. Because I was experienced at speaking things into existence and calling things that be not as though they were, I went ahead and gave thanks for my current level of abundance and for an increased level of abundance. I now understood why God had urged me to pray for an abundant mindset rather than just money. It's the old parable that says "If you feed a man a fish, he will eat for a day. If you teach him to fish, he will eat for a lifetime". God was teaching me to fish by teaching me to develop the mindset and mental capacity to create abundance from within. He knew that once I had an abundant mindset, I would be able to attract whatever I needed on my own. Had He simply honored my request for more money, it would have only changed my circumstances temporarily and I would have missed out on the bigger lesson. Abundance comes from within and when we speak, see, and live from a state of abundance, we cannot help but become a magnet for all that we desire. Furthermore, I could see how my poverty and scarcity mindset had been at work throughout my entire life. I had a low financial setpoint and a poor capacity to receive.

Since I have been working to change my mindset from scarcity to abundance and shift from a poverty consciousness to a wealth consciousness, I have seen my financial life make drastic improvements. I no longer sit and beg God to fix my situation or give me more money. I now create those images in my mind and use the power of my word, my thoughts, my imagination and my beliefs to create my experiences. It is not that I no longer need God, but I now understand and accept that God has given us the power to create wealth and that as a man thinketh, so is he. Abundance is our birthright and our natural state of being. When we truly change our mindsets and accept that abundance is all there is, we see that there is no such thing as not enough or just enough. In reality, there is an abundance of everything such as water, oxygen, and vegetation. Lack and scarcity are only illusions and ones we can either accept or ignore. I understand that for some people, your reality may be showing you evidence of lack, scarcity, poverty, and not enough. Maybe you feel if you had more money, more opportunity, more support or more resources, things would get better and I am sure they would temporarily. But if you can work to overcome this past mental conditioning and begin to adopt an abundant mindset and wealth consciousness, you would see your circumstances begin to change before your eyes. We have all heard the old saying that the rich get richer and the poor get poorer. The reality is that the rich get richer not just because they are lucky or dishonest, but because of their rich mindset. The poor stay poor because of their poor mindset. We are what we believe and what we think about most of the time. If we are always focusing on not enough, lack and scarcity, then that is exactly what we will continue to experience. If we start to shift our focus to plenty and abundance, we will begin to attract those experiences into our lives as well. We have to stop speaking and giving life with our words to what we don't want, and start speaking life to what we do want. How many times have you overheard someone complaining about bills, expenses and the lack of money? If you follow that person for the next few months, you will continue to watch them undergo similar experiences. It is the same with people who constantly complain about their relationships, their physical health or their jobs. The more we focus and tune into the things we do not want, the more life gives us of those same experiences. We reap what we sow. When we sow thoughts, words and beliefs in lack, we reap lack. When we sow thoughts of abundance, plenty and enough, we will eventually reap those as well. Sometimes it takes a while for things to turn around because we may have been stuck in our current situation a long time, but "Let us not grow weary in doing good, for in due season, we will reap a harvest if we faint not".

Awareness

Even though, I was somewhat familiar with the concept of *awareness* before writing this book and had my own working definition of it, I can honestly say I now have a much deeper level of understanding. Awareness is defined as the ability to directly know and perceive, to feel, to be conscious of or cognizant. Being aware is not simply having knowledge of something, but being tuned into what is around and within us. In meditation, we are often guided to become aware of our breath which helps us to limit distractions and keep our thoughts from wandering. Awareness is the intentional action of paying attention, focusing and tuning in. Just as I shared earlier about abundance being something we tune into". Essentially, abundance is all around us and we only see or experience lack and scarcity because that is what we are tuned into. When I had my aha moment with that statement and began to take note of all the abundance in my life and the world around me, it changed everything and I decided to apply this same concept to other areas of my life such as my health, happiness, and peace. We are finally learning that happiness is something we cannot purchase, achieve or acquire, but something we choose to be and tune into, especially when we operate from the belief that what we desire already exists and is simply awaiting our recognition and awareness of it.

The Law of Attraction states that what we focus on expands, so if we focus all of our attention on good health, we will attract the things and situations necessary to experience good health, but if we focus all of our attention on sickness or even our fear of some disease, then we are more likely to attract and develop illness and disease. You may wonder, "Who would ever focus on sickness or poverty or disaster?" The reality is, many of us focus on those things everyday through our negative thoughts, doubts, worries, fears and beliefs. For example, doctors have often noted how rapidly a person's health deteriorates and their condition worsens after they are diagnosed with a disease. They may have had the disease for years and not known it, but the moment their attention is brought to it and they begin to talk about it, Google it, worry about it, stress over it and focus on it, their condition worsens. Likewise, if we focus on not getting a job, being broke and poor, unhappy, alone, and any number of other ills, our attention and awareness is on those things and we are expanding and attracting them to us. I do want to clarify that choosing to focus our attention on health is not the same as pretending an illness or disease does not exist. We can be aware that sickness exists, but still choose to focus on health and wellness. We can be aware that there is poverty in the world, hunger, terrorism, hatred, racism, wars, and disaster all around us and still choose to focus on the good that exists in the world. So, if you truly need to seek medical attention, continue to take those steps in the natural to help bring about your healing but keep your focus on being well. If you have limited finances, focus on wealth, but continue to live within your means until your wealth shows up.

I now believe we have a choice in where and how to focus our attention; therefore, we can make a conscious, deliberate decision to focus our attention and thoughts on health, wealth, abundance, happiness and peace. This does not mean we will not ever get sick, have financial issues or days when we feel sad or unhappy, but if it is a choice either way, then let us "meditate on the higher things of the spirit" and shift our awareness off of what we do not want and onto the things that cause us to feel more optimistic and inspired.

Personal Reflection:

1) Are you living from an abundant or a poverty mindset? Remember abundance is not just money. Abundance is time, health, happiness and fulfilling relationships.

2) Make a list of all the tangible forms of money in your life, from the dollar stuck in your coat pocket to the money in a life insurance policy or jar of coins. What did you discover?

3) Now make a list of all intangible forms of income.

4) If your mindset shifted from lack and scarcity to abundance and wealth, how might that change your situation? Your life?

5) How will it benefit you to become more aware and tuned into in your life?

Chapter 21

Give it All Away

"No one has ever become poor by giving"
~~Anne Frank

I can still recall the exact day when I heard God say, "Give it all away". I literally felt my body and mind go into panic mode as my first thought became, "But God, if I give it all away, I won't have anything left. I'll be broke, without, and lacking". I decided to meditate on it. Surely, I thought, God didn't mean "all". A few days later, I heard it again. "Give it all away". I asked God what He meant when He said all (as if all has a different meaning from "all") and it was then that the understanding manifested inside of me as I began to realize that we can never really own anything. Sadly, we have bought into the illusion that we can, but the reality is that we enter the world owning and possessing nothing except the air in our lungs, and we leave here without even that. Sure, we may acquire and accumulate property and other possessions in life that are ours to enjoy for the duration of time we have them, but eventually those things are passed along to someone else from the car we trade in to the home we sell, clothes we donate, and the jewelry we lose that someone else finds. All of the things we attach to and hold dear will ultimately end up with someone else. Owning them is temporary and transitory.

I remember once seeing an email showing a wealthy man being buried in an underground room complete with a bed, television and other luxuries. While this may seem shocking and unbelievable, many of us actually live life holding onto things and possessions as if we too will somehow end up taking them with us into the afterlife. This is commonly referred to as "attachment". We develop strong attachments to our "stuff" to the point of experiencing intense emotions and feelings of anxiety and panic at the thought of releasing them, losing them, or giving them away. The reality TV show, *Hoarders*, is a great example of people who have attached themselves to things in such a way that it has become disordered and problematic; however, it is not only the people who are living with mounds of trash in their homes that struggle with attachment. Most of us do on some level. We attach to our relationships, certain foods, clothing, cars, homes, our physical appearance, and our social or economic status up to the point where we panic when we're faced with the threat of losing those things.

Years ago, my mother made the down payment on a brand-new Ford Mustang as my college graduation gift. I fell in love with that car. It was a beautiful shade of blue and had a five-disc CD changer which was the hot new thing at the time. I felt so amazing when I drove my new car and everyone complimented me on it. I kept it for five years and even took it with me when I moved to NYC and later to Atlanta. After a while, I began to have issues with my beautiful car and soon discovered that the engine was about to go out. I desperately needed a car fast and I ended up trading in my beautiful Mustang one weekend for a car I did not love. I can still remember the moment I understood that I was leaving my beloved car behind and driving away with this new car, and it brought tears to my eyes. I literally felt a profound sense of separation and loss…from a car! I thought about the dealership fixing the engine and selling the car, my car, to someone else and me seeing them driving around town in it. It took a few months for me to finally let go and accept that my beautiful blue Mustang was no longer mine. At the time, I did not fully grasp or understand that life is meant to be a continual process of ebb and flow. In the chapter on flow, I discussed that it is essential for us to operate in flow if we are to live and enjoy our best lives. When we possess, attach, cling and hoard, we block flow and inhibit the process of circulation and movement that is inherent in the universe. My initial reaction of panic and anxiety to God saying "give it all away" was triggered by my internal fear of loss, and a belief in lack and deprivation that me "giving it all away", would cause me to end up broke and empty. This fear of loss and belief in lack goes against the spiritual Law of Abundance which states that there is no such thing as lack or scarcity. In fact, there is more than enough and you and I have no need to own or possess anything. Again, we can fully enjoy and take care of what we are blessed with as long as we maintain an understanding that one day it will belong to someone else and that we will not lose, we will simply give, share or transfer it. Because the universe hates a vacuum (empty space), it will replace that thing with someone or something that better serves who and where we are in that time and space.

Furthermore, I have been studying the Law of Attraction for several years and I believe that what we give out or give away always comes back to us; The Law of Karma says that our words, thoughts and deeds (positively or negatively) create a corresponding energy that comes back to us in one form or another; and of course, the Bible speaks about the principle of sowing and reaping and how if we sow (give, share) sparingly, we will also reap (receive) sparingly. If we sow bountifully, we will reap bountifully. I slowly began to understand how my willingness to give was the very definition of generosity and abundance and I could clearly see how my fear and belief had previously affected my ability to let things go, as in the example of my car. I began to realize that my willingness to give it all away literally makes me a partner with the universe and as I am willing to serve God and the world by giving and sharing, the universe becomes even more willing to serve and give back to me. It is an amazing relationship to have and I have truly seen my life change as a result of this mindset shift.

In reality, I have always been a giver. I have paid for people's groceries and gas and supported less fortunate children and families during the holidays. I have even left cash inside of envelopes in people's mailboxes as a "surprise". Although this always felt natural to me, inwardly I still struggled with fears of lack and scarcity and would never have considered giving it all away.

When I began to understand and accept that I cannot lose anything and that everything is in circulation and will eventually come back around in some other form, it helped me to become more willing to let things go and not hoard and cling to stuff. Now, have I given away my home, my possessions, all my savings, and my relationships? I would like to think so, but no. I am not there yet. What I have done is become more willing to give freely and bountifully of my time, talent and treasure whenever the opportunity presents itself.

I do not think we should give out of obligation, nor should we try to be God in someone else's life because doing so says to the universe that we believe in lack for them. I give for the blessing, the privilege and the sake of giving without attachment or expectation. I give because of how it makes me feel and because of how it enriches me, enlarges me, expands me, serves the world, demonstrates my trust in the universe and supports my belief that the windows of Heaven are always open.

Personal Reflection:

1) What are you holding onto or hoarding that may be causing you distress? It can be a possession, a relationship, a job, a home, a habit, etc.

2) How would your life be different if you began to give and share the best of you without hesitation or expectation?

3) How can you adopt and operate in flow?

4) Where are you not allowing circulation or flow in your life?

Chapter 22

Make Your Requests Known

"Ask and it will be given to you"
~~Matthew 7:7

Making our requests known is about developing the ability to ask for what we want and need, but also learning how to accept and receive the things we have asked for. This is a concept that took me years to finally grasp because for much of my life, I struggled with asking and receiving. As I mentioned in the previous chapter, I have always been pretty good at giving, but I was terrible at asking for what I wanted and needed and I now believe that our giving and receiving should be as balanced as our breathing. Because I grew up with a single mother who earned minimum wage and yet never asked for or accepted government assistance in any form, her pride and work ethic taught me that it was not okay to ask for what I needed nor was it okay to expect help or receive from others. In fact, receiving was viewed as charity and I felt like my mother wanted us to know that just because we did not have a lot of money, that did not mean we were inferior. The truth was, there were times when I felt inferior to my friends and classmates whose families had more money, but this was also when I decided that I would grow up, be successful and become a millionaire. I decided I would prove to everyone that I was not less than, inadequate, poor or inferior. What I did not realize though is how my attitude and pride became barriers to asking and receiving and not only did I have issues around receiving money, I had issues with receiving in general. I had watched my mother on countless occasions refuse help from others even for something as simple as accepting gas money from someone to whom she had given a ride. I learned that asking was a bad thing. I learned that I have to do it all myself, stand on my own two feet and not need anyone. While these were great qualities and attributes to have in many ways, they have also crippled me in a lot of others.

I am a multi-talented person with several business endeavors, two young children, a husband and a household; yet I have rarely asked for help from family, friends or others. From 2015 to 2020, I rented a gorgeous 2000+ square foot office and I can remember feeling a sense of pride at my willingness to clean the building myself because my budget did not allow for me to hire a cleaning company. I was the therapist, office assistant, receptionist, billing specialist, housekeeper and even the exterminator. When I think back over my work history, I have always been that person, the one who felt the need to "do it all" and do it all myself. Even when I had assistants or employees, I would end up doing most of their duties because of their inability or unwillingness to do them. Like my mother, I refused to accept charity, refused to ask for help and continued living my life like some superwoman in charge of saving the world.

I even perpetuated this do-it-all-myself attitude in my relationships with men, my female friendships and within my family. I planned our trips, family reunions, dates, etc. On one hand, I understood that I am a leader and have been gifted with certain skills and talents, but knowing what I know now, I feel so much sympathy and compassion for the woman that I was. The woman who believed that she had to do everything and do it all herself. The woman who thought she had something to prove. It was in 2018 when I truly came to grips with my issues around asking for money and assistance. Someone had listened to my talk radio show and sent me a text message congratulating me. After a few texts back and forth, she asked me if I had cash app or a donate button on my website. I had neither. She then told me to immediately add a donate button on my website and download the cash app. Within a matter of minutes, she sent me $200. I was shocked and in awe. I thanked her and then called my sister and told her what happened. Not surprisingly, she admitted she too struggled with asking for money (after all, we did grow up in the same home). After that day, I began to pray and seek guidance in this area and I finally started to understand where this false sense of humility and independence had originated. It wasn't just the fact of being raised by my fiercely independent mother. I had to admit that deep down, it also came from a feeling of not believing I deserved to ask and receive or have things be easy for me, and from a sense of pride that I did not want anyone to think I was needy or less than them. Once I recognized this, I owned it and I decided right then and there to do the work to overcome this. It is amazing how life begins to show up and offer us unlimited opportunities to grow when we become willing to face and overcome something.

Interestingly, I was not unfamiliar with the concept of people having issues with asking and receiving. I work with clients all the time who struggle with the same thing. I just did not realize how deep my own sense of guilt and pride went when it came to asking for money and assistance. I thought back over all of the events and businesses I had become involved in where I never made much money. I would go into each new venture filled with excitement and a sense of purpose and end up walking away discouraged having lost money or not made very much of it. My excuse became that I was not a salesperson. In fact, I disliked salespeople and saw them as dishonest, manipulative and untrustworthy. I told myself if God or someone else wanted me to have something, they would just give it me. I told myself that if I just continued to be a good person, pay my tithes, and give freely to others, then everything would be "added unto me". I believed that the windows of Heaven would open up and pour out blessings on me when I had sacrificed enough, worked hard and proven myself worthy and deserving enough. I knew the Bible said to ask and it shall be given and I also knew it said, "Be anxious for nothing, but in everything, by prayer and supplication, with thanksgiving, make your requests known to God" in addition to numerous other references about asking and receiving. I understood that we get what we expect, but because I felt unworthy and underserving, when I did ask, I half expected not to receive it. I felt guilty for asking and I felt weak, needy, and inferior. Thank God for understanding and awareness, because what I have now discovered is that our worthiness and deservingness is not based on the presence or lack of money or resources. I have come to understand and believe that we are worthy and deserving just because of who we are and because we are. Asking for what we need and want is not evidence or a demonstration of our lack, inferiority, neediness or inadequacy; actually, it is the opposite. As a result of this revelation, I now ask with expectation, knowing I am worthy and deserving of receiving. If someone says no or chooses not to give, I know that it is not an indication of my worth or value and I simply ask someone else. I now expect great things to happen for me. I expect people to give to me, serve me, support me, assist me and pay me what I charge. I understand now why I was having such terrible luck before. It wasn't that my business sense wasn't good or my ideas were not lucrative. It wasn't that God didn't favor me or that people were hating on me or rejecting me, it was my pride that had prevented me from asking with an expectation of receiving. It was my need to prove myself and my unresolved feelings of guilt. It was my feelings of unworthiness and my own inner sense of lack and inadequacy. In the book of James, we are told that we have not, because we ask not. We are also told to give. But the truth is we have to be willing and able to receive and know we are worthy of receiving. Honestly, who are we not to expect God's blessings and goodness? Yes, we may have to face and let go of pride, guilt and condemnation. We may have to forgive ourselves and other people. We may have to overcome things from the past that have convinced us of who we are not and of what we do not deserve. In the end, asking and expecting to receive demonstrates our worthiness, our belief and understanding that if we do not receive from one area or person, it is not a personal reflection of us. I fully recognize that God is our unlimited source of good. He supplies everything we need and if the door closes, it simply wasn't our door and according to the Law of Abundance, another will open that is better for us. I am learning to trust that God and life will cause things to bend in my favor and lean in my direction. I now ask, already knowing that the moment I ask, it is given unto me. "Even before you call, I shall answer". The *how* is not our concern. Our job is simply to ask, believe, and receive.

Personal Reflection:

1) Do you struggle with asking and/or receiving? If so, can you identify why and how this began?

2) What do you desire that you are still afraid or unwilling to ask for?

3) How would learning to give and receive equally benefit you?

Chapter 23

Being Seen & Showing Up

"Vulnerability is about showing up and being seen. It's tough to do that when we're terrified about what people might see or think"
~~Brine' Brown

At some point, we all may have to face and overcome the fear of being seen and showing up. This fear may present in a variety of ways and numerous areas, many of which we may not even be aware. Regardless of whether we recognize it or not, the fear of being seen and showing up prevents countless numbers of people from ever achieving their full potential in life. Perhaps underneath the fear of being seen and showing up is the fear of being revealed or exposed as a fraud, imposter, or not good enough. Because so many of us are hiding who we really are, we may believe that if we can fade into the background and remain hidden and unseen, there is less chance of being exposed, which leaves us open and susceptible to criticism, attack, rejection or injury. For many people who have been emotionally wounded in life, the need to hide and the fear of being seen becomes a defense mechanism and a tool for self-sabotage. People with a fear of being seen and showing up may wonder why they struggle with procrastination or why they are consistently late to meetings and appointments. They may tell themselves they are more comfortable in the background and have no need or desire for the spotlight, often while hiding behind their limitations or responsibilities. They may also hide behind their friends, children, spouses, addictions, and even their own bodies. I have had several clients reveal to me that losing weight made them feel exposed, naked, vulnerable, and unsafe. They admit to sabotaging their weight loss and regaining the weight in order to feel safe, protected and covered again. Research has shown that a lot of people will subconsciously gain extra weight in their midsection because it becomes a protective barrier and covering. This is especially true of people who have been sexually abused and assaulted. Many of my clients who were sexually abused admit to believing that being heavy will make them less attractive and desirable which they believe will prevent further violation. The truth is that we all sometimes hide, shrink or attempt to blend in for a variety of reasons. But in order to become whole, authentic and live our best lives, we are going to have to face our fears and give ourselves permission to come out of hiding and be seen.

I have always stood out, even though not all of those reasons have been good. I was the only child in my family to never meet our father, I was the only Black student in most of my classes in elementary school, I was the only Black girl in my class competing for Miss Sophomore, Miss Junior and Miss Senior, and I was the only Black student to speak at my high school graduation along with the valedictorian, salutatorian and class president. I was even the mascot for our high school band when I was only five years old. Looking back, I can see that one of the best things my mother did for me was to involve me in activities that forced me to speak up, stand up and be seen which has served me well in many arenas; however, standing out and being seen has also come along with many challenges. Standing out in school sometimes meant that my Black classmates thought I was too smart and didn't fit in, while some of my white classmates questioned how I was smart enough to be in the same classes with them. As an adult, standing out has caused some of the people around me to feel intimidated, insecure and inadequate which has also caused them to reject me, abandon me, or attack me. Standing out at work caused my supervisor at my last job to feel threatened to the point where she began to micromanage me and nitpick in her efforts to discredit and prevent me from being promoted over her.

While standing out has often been a blessing in my life, it has also brought a lot of discomfort especially because of my longstanding need to prove myself and be liked. I realize now that I have often looked for ways to hide, blend in and shrink as I tried to conform to other people's opinions and ways of thinking. I have gone along to get along and agreed to things that were against my true beliefs. I hid who I really was, and at one point, my true self became almost invisible. I even created a representative of myself that I believed would be more acceptable, likeable, agreeable, and would not stand out too much or outshine anyone else. Sadly, no matter how much I tried to shrink, conform and hide, I still never found a true sense of belonging and instead of standing out, I felt like I was always "sticking out" which only caused me to shrink back even further. Eventually, I withdrew and concealed my gifts and talents and kept the best parts of myself hidden from everyone except my husband and children.

It wasn't until I published my first book that I could no longer hide because my book had exposed me in such a way that made it nearly impossible to shrink. In it, I revealed my worst childhood secrets and my struggles with low self-esteem and daddy issues. Ironically though, my story endeared me to people and instead of them criticizing and rejecting me as I had feared, they were drawn to me. While I was enjoying the attention and recognition on the outside, those hidden parts on the inside of me were still living in fear of being exposed because they were afraid that I was going to be too visible and stand out way too much which would invite injury, assault, criticism and attack. What I really feared though was that people would see behind my mask and discover that I was really broken, unworthy, defective, inadequate, inferior, ugly, lacking and not good enough. I am so grateful to God for my healing and revealing the truth to me about me that when I fully accept me, and make peace with my past, I will never have to worry about anyone else exposing me or discovering that I am a fraud, an imposter or a fake. I can love and accept myself wholeheartedly. This self-acceptance and no longer having to prove myself has given me permission to be my true self and to rise to my full stature without bending, shrinking or hiding out of fear of intimidating, threatening or outshining anyone.

Beauty

In addition to overcoming the fear of being seen, we may also have to address our internal and external concept of beauty. Coco Chanel famously stated that "Beauty begins the moment you decide to be yourself". From 1996-2007, I owned a private label cosmetics company that I named Silhouette Cosmetics. The focus of my brand was on enhancing natural beauty and my company slogan was "Beauty isn't what you see, it's how you see it". What sounded like a great marketing scheme then, is the basis of many life lessons for me now. Beauty is not just what we see, it is how we see it.

Perhaps, I did not learn the true meaning of this until I started working with clients who were struggling with their internal concept of beauty. Early in my counseling practice, I was working with a young female client who had a face that could literally stop traffic. I remember thinking she could easily grace the cover of any national magazine and yet this beautiful, young girl struggled with very unhealthy body image and self-esteem issues that had developed into an eating disorder as a result of her self-loathing. She had also been in numerous abusive relationships and had attempted suicide because of how undesirable she felt. I remember thinking to myself, "Can she not see what I see"? This client taught me that it really doesn't matter how pretty you appear to someone else, if you do not see it within yourself, it is meaningless. She also taught me that when you feel ugly and unattractive on the inside, your outer appearance ceases to matter. Since then I have gone on to work with countless other clients who have felt ugly and unattractive within and it has also helped to me to address and overcome my own struggles.

As a child, I was always considered pretty and I can remember going places with my mother and overhearing older people tell her I was "the prettiest child she had". It was also during those times that I would also hear my mother reply, "pretty is as pretty does" which gave me sort of a mixed message about beauty. I felt beautiful and enjoyed the advantages that came along with it, and then there were times when I wanted to hide my face when someone stared at me or called me beautiful. Beauty had always made me stand out and be seen; beauty helped me measure up; and beauty had gotten me nominated to be in my high school pageant three times. However, beauty was not always a good thing and I remember my cousin Erica once telling me that beauty could be both a blessing and a curse. I never understood what she meant at the time, but eventually I began to see firsthand when I started to sense that some of my friends were afraid of me stealing their boyfriends. Beauty was also the "reason" I was given by my two male cousins to explain why they had molested me. Outside of that, beauty was a blessing that caused people to be nice to me and beauty made me feel good about myself because I was able to hide all of my shortcomings and insecurities behind my appearance; later, I would discover that beauty had also helped me cover up and avoid the places inside of me that felt undesirable, inadequate, unattractive, and downright ugly.

I don't think I truly learned what real beauty was until I began to feel not so beautiful around age 46. At that time, what once seemed so natural and easy for me now took effort to achieve. I found myself spending extra time doing my make-up and often admiring women with flawless skin who did not need to wear foundation or concealer. It was then that I started to realize I could no longer hide behind or depend on my external appearance to make me feel good inside. I knew I would have to discover a sense of beauty that went beyond skin deep and address the things at my core that made me feel unattractive.

The 90's hip hop group TLC released a song entitled, *Unpretty*, which says we can wear makeup, add hair or get plastic surgery to fix ourselves on the outside, but we have to look inside to find and discover who we are. When we don't, we allow other people's ideas, opinions and words to cause us to feel unattractive and ugly on the inside. So many of us, especially women, struggle to overcome a negative self-concept and poor self-image because of our internal feelings about beauty. As young girls and older women, we are constantly bombarded with unrealistic external standards of beauty by other people from the music and fashion industry to the media. Young girls are bullied online and offline about their height, weight, hair, skin, teeth, and overall appearance. People who are overweight are fat-shamed and celebrities who do not immediately "snap back" to their original weight after pregnancy are ridiculed. It is no wonder why so many of us struggle to have a healthy self-image and why we have people going to such horrific lengths to achieve what they consider beautiful, from developing eating disorders to dangerous butt injections by unqualified individuals.

When I am with clients who are having issues in this area, instead of handing them all mirrors and attempting to reassure them of the beauty I see on the outside, I work with them on healing the negative self-concept, perception and image they may have of themselves on the inside. Self-image is how we see ourselves in relation to others. Self-concept is our awareness and understanding of ourselves. If we see ourselves as good, worthy, deserving, adequate and complete, we will most likely have a very positive self-concept and self-image and we will engage in healthy behaviors, activities and relationships. We also will not rely so heavily on other people's opinions of us. On the other hand, if we see ourselves as ugly, lacking, unworthy, not good enough, defective or bad, then we are more likely to have a negative self-image and self-concept and we will constantly seek other people's reassurance, validation, approval and acceptance. Because how we see and perceive ourselves is largely based on what we believe about ourselves, we can make unlimited changes to our outer appearance and still feel hideous and unattractive on the inside. Perhaps this explains why weight loss surgery clients are required to undergo psychological assessments before and after surgery, because despite having reduced their weight by tens or hundreds of pounds, they may still see themselves as the fat person in the mirror. In the movie, Central Intelligence, Dwayne "The Rock" Johnson plays the role of an overweight high school boy who was often teased and bullied about his weight. During the last school assembly of his senior year, he ends up being exposed and humiliated in front of the entire student body. Years later, he reappears lean and chiseled; however, when he is confronted by the same bully from high school who had treated him the worst, he could no longer see what he had become and instead still saw the same fat kid inside of him. There is an actual scene in the movie where he looks at his reflection and sees himself as he was in high school. The truth is that what we believe about ourselves and how we see and perceive ourselves is a central theme of everything in life because it will determine what careers we pursue, what jobs we apply for, or our decision to go after the things we desire. It will determine the types of friends we have and the relationships we enter, and it will also determine how we speak up and show up. What we believe about ourselves will ultimately determine our degree of self-worth, self-esteem and self-confidence.

Beauty is in the eye of the beholder and we will not be everyone's cup of tea any more than everyone will be our cup of tea, but we must continue to develop a healthy self-image and self-concept, so that we can always see and appreciate ourselves in the best light possible.

Personal Reflection:

1) In what ways have you failed to show up for you?

2) In what ways are you still shrinking, hiding and holding back for fear of being exposed?

3) What have you not accepted about yourself that you fear someone might discover about you?

4) Have you ever felt unwanted, undesirable or unpretty? If so, think back to who or what may have caused you to feel this way and make a list of names.

5) What do you need to release in order for your true beauty to shine through?

Chapter 24

The Possibility Zone

"Do one thing every day that scares you"
~~Eleanor Roosevelt

The comfort zone is often described as a place of comfort or familiarity, and it involves a certain level of safety and control. In grade school and college, I can recall how my classmates and I would enter a new class and choose a seat either near the people we knew, or that served some other purpose such as being near the exit While we may have changed seats a couple of times in those first few days, eventually, we ended up sitting in the same chair/section for the remainder of the semester/quarter.

Human beings are regularly referred to as creatures of habit. A creature of habit is defined as a person who follows an unwavering routine or pattern. I would also add that human beings are creatures of comfort which means we like things that bring us a certain level of comfort and familiarity. It may be that we believe there is a degree of safety and control in things we know and have become accustomed to. The definition of comfort is a state of ease, or freedom from pain or constraint. The comfort zone is defined as a psychological state in which things feel familiar to a person and they are at ease and in control of their environment with low levels of stress, pain and anxiety. We like the comfort zone and we often gravitate towards the things, people and places that feel safe, predictable and familiar to us. We like comfort foods, comfortable spaces to live and work, comfortable clothing and comfortable relationships with people we know and like. We even like comfort in our bodies, which is why some of us struggle with exercise or losing weight. Sadly, it is our same desire and need for comfort and familiarity that keeps us trapped in abusive or unfulfilling relationships, unhealthy patterns of behavior such as addiction, overeating, poverty, obesity, illness, and incarceration. We get used to situations that do not feel safe and do not feel good, and we forget that we really are not stuck, trapped or constrained…except in our thinking. Unfortunately, we are sometimes willing to deal with the discomfort of an undesirable or unsafe situation simply because it is familiar rather than the discomfort of facing the unknown, the unpredictable and the unfamiliar. What is interesting to me is that as children, we could not wait to explore the unknown. We looked forward to new toys and games, developing new abilities, visiting new places, meeting new people, discovering new adventures and finding new ways of doing things. We welcomed opportunities to grow and yet somehow along the way, we developed a fear of the unknown and began to seek out what was comfortable, familiar and predictable in order to maintain a sense of control and safety. By holding on to what is familiar, predictable and comfortable, we not only keep ourselves tied to things that may no longer serve us, we also inhibit and prevent ourselves from discovering what lies outside of the comfort zone. Going back to when we were children and full of wonder, excitement and amazement, we sought out ways to go beyond our comfort zones or at least expand them. As adults, we may discover that going outside of our comfort zones provides us with similar life-changing opportunities for wonder, excitement and amazement, and it also opens us up to discover new abilities, strengths, places, interests, likes, dislikes, preferences, and endless possibilities. We live in an abundant universe that is filled with rich, exciting experiences just waiting to provide us with new ways to grow, evolve, and expand. Yes, it is scary, unfamiliar, and unpredictable, but so were all of our other experiences in the very beginning. Yes, there are going to be risks involved, but let us remember that we came here to this unknown place called earth, without any prior knowledge or experience, and yet we were open to life and everything it had to offer. Unfortunately, we may have experienced some pain, rejection, neglect, hurt, or abuse that made us close ourselves off and seek safety and comfort over adventure and exploration. Our ancestors knew that if a thing is not constantly growing and evolving, it is dying which I believe is what inspired them to become pioneers in search of distant lands and faraway places. That same spirit is still alive on the inside of every one of us. Outside the comfort zone, a world of opportunity and possibility exists and awaits us. Outside of the comfort zone, mystery, magic and miracles are waiting. Outside of the comfort zone, life is waiting to provide us with the tools, resources, information, insight, and everything else we need to fulfill our purpose in life.

Personal Reflection:

1) Are you trapped in a comfort zone that may not feel comfortable, but not familiar?

2) What are three things you can begin doing immediately to help you expand your degree or comfort and stretch outside of that familiar zone?

Chapter 25

Do You Believe in Magic?

"Those who don't believe in magic will never find it"
Roald Dahl

Getting out of our comfort zones and into our possibility zones will certainly help us to believe in magic again. As I reflect back on my childhood, I can honestly say that I believed in magic; not just magic from the standpoint of trickery and illusions, but magic in the sense that anything was possible and magic in the sense of my imagination and my mind's ability to create incredible stories, ideas and fantasies. I had (and still have) a love for reading and I found so much magic inside the books I read; magic that could bend time, make the invisible visible, and help someone triumph in cases of extreme adversity. Yes, I believed in magic and I believed there was magic inside of me. Again, I am not referring to an ability to pull a rabbit out of a hat, but I believed that if there was magic in the world, then it also must have existed in me. I believed that the magic inside of me had the power to help me overcome insurmountable odds and triumph over tragedy. As an adult, I still have a fascination about the world and I enjoy being able to share magical, mystical experiences with my children. My children also believe in magic and that all things are possible. They are readers and we love reading together and creating things together. I always encourage them to use their imaginations and stretch their minds far and wide. This comes easy to them. Actually, it comes easy to most children. I believe that children are born believing without the need for concrete evidence. In fact, children look for reasons to believe and they seek evidence to prove their beliefs are real. I can still recall me and my siblings trying our best to stay awake and catch a glimpse of Santa Claus on Christmas Eve. We were not looking to prove he didn't exist; we were looking for evidence that he did! As adults we look for reasons NOT to believe and find all sorts of ways to explain why great things are happening to us or why our magical experiences are "mere coincidences". Without even realizing it, we steal the magic away from children the same way ours was stolen from us and we replace it with worry, doubt and fear. Slowly, children begin to question the very existence of magic and eventually, they too stop believing.

One night as I was lying in bed unable to sleep, I started searching for information on all of this while asking myself, "Why do we stop believing? What happens to us as we age and mature?" During my searching, I came across an eBook entitled, "Awakening the Genius Within". In it, the author stated that whenever he asks a group of five-year-old children how many of them are geniuses, every hand in the room goes up. When he continues up the grade levels, by the time he reaches high school children, one or no hands are raised. Why is that? Maybe, we can attribute this to the innocence or ignorance of childhood and say that children do not know any better or do not even understand the meaning of the word genius. What I do know is that if anyone had asked me if I was a genius as a child or if I believed in magic, I would have immediately said yes without fear or doubt. What is it I knew or felt then that shifted in me as I grew and developed? Of course, I can certainly see how negative life experiences changed my thinking, but I also believe that some of it came from socialization. Interestingly, the more we develop and rely on the acceptance of our peers or anyone outside of ourselves, the more we begin to adopt beliefs that are socially acceptable and safe, even if they go against the truth of what we believe inside. After all, no one wants to be laughed at or ridiculed for still believing in magic after a certain age. And while I am not advocating that we should believe in magic in the aspect of illusion, I can state without hesitation or doubt that my faith was a lot stronger when I did believe and my ability to trust without questioning was much greater. If we think about it, we must believe in a little bit of magic to be able to accept and believe in the miracles of Jesus. Otherwise, if it is all science, logic or human intellect, then we must also question the feeding of the five thousand, the water being turned to wine, Peter walking on water and Lazarus being raised from the dead. All of these occurrences defy gravity and intellect and yet we are willing to accept that they happened. Or are we? When we truly study the miracles in the Bible, there are countless examples of things that go against what is logical and scientific. I was recently speaking to a friend who was starting to tap into her spirituality and as a result, she was beginning to have experiences that appeared to be coincidental, except that they kept happening. When she could not explain them away, she reached out to me for insight. I shared with her my belief that since we are spiritual beings in human form, it is highly conceivable that we will have spiritual experiences and not just in a church or other religious institution. This caused me to ask myself, "Why is it that we claim to believe in a supernatural God we cannot see, believe that He created the entire universe in six days, and yet question all of it when supernatural things happen to us?" Why do those things frighten us or make us look for ways to explain it? Why do we look for reasons NOT to believe instead of looking for evidence that we CAN believe? Imagine how our lives would change if we actively looked for reasons to believe and have faith, instead of the other way around. Even though we have an area of the brain that is focused on logic, reason, and intellect, we do not have to always give in to the ego and question our supernatural ability. It is who we are! We were created In God's own image and likeness; how can we NOT have supernatural abilities and expect to experience miracles and magic on a regular basis?!

One day while writing this book, my husband shared with me an excerpt from a book he was reading by Kim Kiyosaki that said we all have genius or a genie-in-us. How incredible does life become when we embrace and accept this? How sad would it be to get to the end of your life only to discover that you had magic and genius within you all along and never tapped into it because you stopped believing, (which came naturally to you), and started living in doubt and fear?

I want to end with one of my favorite quotes by Marianne Williamson that says "Our deepest fear is not that we are inadequate. Our deepest fear is that we are powerful beyond measure. It is our light, not our darkness, that most frightens us". I can honestly say that when my clients begin to discover who they really are and what they are capable of, it seems to both frighten and overwhelm them and I often find myself having to reassure them that it is okay to accept and embody their own greatness. I intend to continue living a supernatural life, expecting to create and experience miracles, mystery, and magic from the belief that anything is possible, because it is.

Personal Reflection:

1) When did you stop believing that anything was possible?

2) Do you believe you have genius inside of you?

3) Have you experienced supernatural things and explained them away as coincidences?

Chapter 26

Unmuted

"It's not what we say out loud that really determines our lives.
It's what we whisper to ourselves that has the most power"
~~Robert T. Kiyosaki

Years ago, when I was living in Brooklyn, NY, I awoke one morning to the sounds of a songbird singing. It was a beautiful lyrical sound and I remember lying there enjoying the purity of it when all of a sudden, a loud, squawking sound began to drown out the beautiful songbird. I felt irritated by it and I kept wishing for it to stop when I realized that God had given voice to the other bird (which I assumed was a crow or a hawk), the same as He did the songbird. I also realized that everything has a voice and a right to be heard, even if the sound is unpleasant, undesirable or not in agreement with those around it. Sadly, many people try to drown out or quiet the voices of other people, and I am reminded of how I have felt muted and in turn, began to quiet my own voice. Growing up, I was always singing, writing poetry and short stories, or practicing my lines for imaginary plays and TV shows in the mirror. I even created a singing group made up of myself and my two youngest siblings. When I was about seven or eight, my oldest sister and I joined the church choir. One Sunday, I lead a solo. I can still see an image of myself holding that microphone and walking around the choir loft until something inside inspired me to walk out into the congregation. Now, the church we attended was NOT a charismatic church. In fact, it was a very conservative church or what some would call a "dead church" and I had never seen anyone walk out of the choir loft into the congregation. However, at that age and time, I did not stop to question whether it was acceptable or okay, I just did what felt natural to me. When I finished my solo, people were standing to their feet, clapping and smiling, and I was beaming inside because I had used my voice and brought joy to other people. In middle and high school, I joined the chorus at school, participated in creative drama and excelled in Language Arts, especially in the area of writing. I also entered and won my high school talent show with two male classmates and became the first female rapper in my hometown. I remember walking the halls feeling ten feet tall. Finally, it seemed, I had found my voice and the courage to use it.

While it seemed was learning to use my voice on the outside, I was struggling to overcome the negative voices on the inside. Not voices that were hallucinatory, but the inner critic voice that almost everyone has inside of them. My inner critic was constantly judging, criticizing, and telling me what I was and what I was not. My negative self-talk was the result of what I believed about myself based on life experiences and other people's views, thoughts and opinions of me. Even though I had enjoyed numerous positive experiences sharing my voice, there had been many negative experiences as well. Living in a town with a lot of racial division meant having to sometimes defend my ethnicity and the way Black people were perceived, especially in terms of language. Being the only or one of only two Black students in most of my advanced level classes meant I was always being questioned or teased about how I sounded or the way I used certain words and phrases. Then there was the fifth-grade spelling bee where I was one of two finalists and I was eliminated because I misspelled the word "abracadabra". I can remember that instead of being congratulated for being a finalist, I was teased for weeks. In my sophomore year of college, my professor gave me a C in my speech class because he said my speeches were too practical and conversational. All of this, along with the shame of my past taught me to quiet my voice and not speak my truth. Subsequently, I learned to say what I thought people wanted to hear when and how they wanted to hear it. I learned how to hold back, dumb down and not speak up for fear of embarrassment, humiliation, or appearing stupid and less intelligent than my peers. I learned that women, Black people and poor people's voices meant less and carried less weight than other people's voices and I learned from my white classmates that I "talk funny". Unfortunately, I allowed all of these negative messages to shape how and when I used my voice and although I continued to speak up and out when necessary, I can admit that I held back and muted myself in a lot of ways. I minimized the truth and watered it down; I didn't speak up and set expectations and boundaries in my relationships, and I allowed people to say hurtful or disrespectful things to me without confrontation. I even allowed people to mispronounce my name without correcting them. I am sure people who know me well are surprised to read this given my current profession as a psychotherapist, life coach, motivational speaker, trainer, author and talk show host, but I am no longer ashamed to admit my struggles and I am no longer afraid to speak my whole truth and nothing but the truth. Partly because I no longer need anyone else's approval or validation, but also because I know there are countless other men and women out there just like me. People who have had their voices silenced, discounted, neglected, unheard and muted. People who have not spoken up and owned their truth. People who have not used their voices to bring about personal or professional change in their lives, families, careers and communities. People who are still holding back and waiting to share their stories of abuse, neglect, heartbreak, betrayal, and hurt, or even their stories of triumph, healing, survival, and transformation.

That morning as I lay in my bed in Brooklyn, I learned that every voice has a right to be heard regardless of age, gender, culture, language, education, social or economic status, or political affiliation The right to speak up and be heard is not just an American privilege granted to us by the constitution, it is a basic human right.

Since my healing journey began, I have become much more intentional in using my voice. When I first started recording my weekly talk radio show, I can remember hating the sound of my own voice. Every time I heard my promo, I would cringe. I would even avoid listening to the playback of the show because a part of me was still remembering how I had been teased and told I "talk funny". I can even remember trying to mimic other people's voices. It is amazing to me now that my voice is my primary source of income. My voice has brought healing, hope, encouragement, motivation, insight, enlightenment, wisdom and understanding to many, and I cannot imagine what would have happened had I decided to hush and allow myself to be muted by others. I now live by a statement expressed by one of my former clients, "No I will not shut up!"

Use Your Words

It is important for us to speak up and use our voices, not only to share our messages and tell our stories, but also so we can learn to use our voices to give life to the things we want for ourselves, such as fulfilling relationships, physical and mental health, financial freedom, and more. The Bible says the power of life and death is in the tongue which means you and I have the ability speak things into existence, and also to bless things and curse things. Not only do we create with our thoughts, beliefs and imagination, but our voices and the words we speak have the power within them to create and/or destroy. The sad part is that many of us have heard this for most of our lives, but we have not really believed it or put it into practice; however, whether we believe it or not, the truth is that our words are constantly creating or destroying the conditions in our lives. Our negative experiences are not just the result of bad luck, bad karma, generational curses, sin, other people or God being angry or disappointed in us. Similarly, our positive experiences are not just the result of good luck, favor, good karma, good deeds or God being pleased with us. We are either speaking life or speaking death and the conditions of our lives become evidence of our words.

In the Bible, we see many examples of the power of words. In Genesis, we read about God speaking the world into creation. We also read about Jesus speaking to the fig tree and causing it to shrivel, Joshua shouting and the Walls of Jericho tumbling to the ground, Paul and Silas praying and singing hymns that caused the prison doors to fly open and everyone's chains to loosen, and countless other examples. I remember my former pastor teaching us about the power of our voices and that we can literally use our words to shift things in the atmosphere. On one occasion, we were expecting a really bad hurricane to make landfall. Usually, we did not worry as much because we lived in the upper part of the state away from the coast, but this particular storm was predicted to come inward and cause destruction to all areas of the state. My pastor had the whole church stand and collectively command the storm to go around us. Now, call it a coincidence, but all I know is that the storm did not do near the damage it was predicted and expected to do.

The truth of the matter is that our words have power. When I was younger, people would often chant "sticks and stones may break my bones, but names will never hurt me". Well as an adult and a psychotherapist, I can emphatically tell you that names and words *do* hurt people. Many of the clients I work with have been deeply hurt by someone's words or names they have been called. I have counseled hundreds of children and adults who were victims of verbal abuse, and I continue to work with people who are still trying to overcome the impact of negative words and statements spoken to them and about them. I witness firsthand the power of words on people who have been called stupid, worthless, dumb, inferior, hopeless, pathetic, insignificant, ugly, and the list goes on. Not to mention the curse words and insults that have been hurled at people by loved ones and enemies alike. In fact, the reason we even use insults and profanity is to hurt, control, and manipulate someone else. Words hurt. And words have power. Words have the power to motivate, inspire, encourage, compliment, express, acknowledge, praise, move, and transform us; they also have the power to belittle, demean, deflate, condescend, wound, and destroy us. Words can change the heart and they can also incite wars and violence. Words can build us up and words can tear us down. Words create the stories we tell and give meaning, color and depth to our lives, language and communication. I once heard Dr. Wayne Dyer speaking on PBS television about how words themselves have a vibration to them. He shared that positive words have a high frequency vibration just as negative words have very low frequency vibrations. We are now realizing that everything in the universe vibrates at different frequencies. People vibrate, animals vibrate, water vibrates, plants and trees vibrate, the earth vibrates, sound and music vibrate and words vibrate. This can help us understand why positive words and statements create positive feelings in us and in others, and why negative words and statements create negative feelings. The reason this is important in helping us live our best lives is because the words we speak and the vibration within those words are creating the circumstances we experience. If prayer and praise can be used to heal sickness and cause storms to cease, then we can use our words to create the lives we want.

Many of the things that have come into existence in my life have been the result of declarations I made aloud to the universe. While I still had to do the work to bring about my desires, the moment I spoke them into the atmosphere, the creation process began. In fact, I spoke my daughter, my husband, my private practice, my first and second home, my radio show, and my books into existence. In January of 2018, I declared that I would be more than a guest at the Essence Festival in July of that year. I had never even been to New Orleans, much less the Essence Festival. I had no celebrity connections, no agent or anything else. I just stood and boldly declared that I would be there. I often joke that by May, I still had not heard from Oprah or the organizers of the festival. A couple of weeks later, my niece tagged me in a post that said they were seeking author submissions for the Festival Bookstore and I immediately knew this was a sign. I submitted my book and waited.

When June came and I still hadn't heard anything, I almost began to doubt myself. That is when I heard God remind me that He is not constrained by time, and all I am required to do is believe. I then began to prepare for my trip. It was literally one week before the event when I received an email informing me that my book had been chosen for the bookstore. My husband and I arranged childcare for our children and we were on the road to New Orleans the following week. I wasn't just lucky and it wasn't magic. I believed God, spoke the word and my word did not return to me void. While I do think I am special, the truth is I am no more special than anyone else when it comes to us using our voices and the power of our words to create the desired circumstances in our lives, instead of using them to destroy our hopes and dreams. We can use our words to build up our children and loved ones, to inspire our partners, to uplift our colleagues, and to comfort and encourage a friend. We can also use the power of our words to speak life into our bodies and our health, our finances, our jobs/careers, relationships and homes. We can use the power of words to pray for others whilst also praising, conversing and communicating with God. It is up to us how we use our words and it is up to us whether we use them to create or destroy. Since everything we speak into the atmosphere comes back to us, it is advisable for us to begin using our words to create and sow as much positive energy and love into ourselves and others as we can.

Self-Talk

Our words are also important when it comes to our self-talk. As a therapist, I usually have to work with clients on improving their self-talk. Self-talk is essentially what it sounds like…how we speak to ourselves. Not just complimenting ourselves when we are dressed to go out on the town or congratulating ourselves for completing a task; self-talk is how we talk to ourselves all of the time. It is what we say to ourselves after a disappointment, a breakup, or a perceived failure. It is what we say to ourselves when we want something we cannot afford or want a position for which we may not feel qualified. It is what we say to ourselves when we make mistakes, do something wrong, or when we feel embarrassed or ashamed. It is even what we say to ourselves when we are angry.

When I started to examine my own self talk, I was amazed to discover how even I, the therapist and the motivational speaker, would speak to my own self at times. I became aware of how negative, critical, condescending and demeaning my self-talk would become when things were not going well or when I felt frustrated. I can tell you; it was anything but loving, patient, kind and understanding. As I continued to explore the concept of self-talk, especially my own, I realized that a lot of our self-talk actually does not even come from us. Sure, we may hear it in our own heads or say it aloud to ourselves, but the origin of some of those very critical, judgmental statements are sometimes the result of something someone else has said to us or about us. As I shared earlier, most of us have an inner critic or a critical parent voice inside of us and if left unchecked, this voice will judge, criticize, demean, and berate us. It will also determine, define and dictate what we say to ourselves and how we say it.

Our self-talk is a great indicator of how we see ourselves and how we feel about ourselves. It reflects our self-esteem, self-confidence and self-image, so it is important for us to examine our self-talk and begin the process of changing it from negative, judgmental and critical to positive, encouraging, and supportive. One of my favorite things to do is look at myself in the mirror and speak directly to me in kind, loving, and supportive ways. I have also begun to redirect my self-talk when I make a mistake, or feel frustrated or embarrassed. In the same ways I want to speak words that build my children, my husband and the people I work with, I also want to make sure I treat myself in a similar manner. In fact, it begins with me. What I learned from speaking more positively to myself is that once I quiet the inner critic inside of me, I find that I am also less critical of others. My self-talk has begun to not only change how I speak *to* myself; it has also changed how I speak *about* myself and it has shifted how I view and feel towards myself. I now use my voice and my words to speak life into me, and I am my own best friend and biggest supporter. I use my voice to motivate and encourage myself, to inspire and uplift, and to nurture and care for myself. It is one of the many ways that I practice self-care and self-love. Believe it or not, this simple practice of changing my self-talk has truly changed the relationship I have with myself. When I look at the woman in the mirror, I no longer fault-find, complain, criticize and analyze. If there is something I want to change, I make the decision to change it or I choose to accept it and love it as it is. I have discovered that loving and accepting ourselves unconditionally is one of the greatest gifts we can give to ourselves, because the more loving and accepting we are of us, the more we are able to genuinely and intentionally show that to others.

If you have ever downplayed, held back, diminished, and muted yourself, remember that all voices are meant to be heard. Speak your truth boldly and intentionally, and use your words to bless your life and the lives of others.

Personal Reflection:

1) What ways have you muted yourself or failed to speak up and use your voice?

2) How would speaking up serve you in life?

3) Are you using your words to bless or curse?

4) How can you become more mindful and speak more intentionally?

5) Is your self-talk positive and uplifting or negative and demeaning?

6) How can you use your self-talk to become more loving and accepting of you?

Chapter 27

A Seat at the Table

"If they don't give you a seat at the table, bring a folding chair"
~~Shirley Chisholm

The book of Samuel mentions a man named Mephibosheth who was the son of Jonathan and the grandson of Saul, both of whom had been killed in battle. In those days, the custom was that if someone's family had been defeated in battle, all remaining members of the family were also killed. Mephibosheth was only five years old when they were both killed and his nurse took him and fled. While she was fleeing, the child either fell or was dropped and could no longer walk afterwards. Years later, when David became king, he sought out any surviving family members from the house of Saul and was informed that Mephibosheth was indeed still alive. Wanting to show kindness to him because of the relationship between him and Mephibosheth's father, Jonathan, David sent for him to be brought to the palace. Not knowing whether he would be killed or not, Mephibosheth went. It is recorded that when David told him of his plans to bless him and restore his land, Mephibosheth, who was struggling with feelings of shame and low self-worth, bowed and compared himself to a dead dog. David then told Mephibosheth that he would always eat at the king's table. Like Mephibosheth, many of us also struggle with those same feelings of shame and low self-worth, which may cause us to feel unworthy and underserving of a seat at the table.

A couple of years ago, I was working with a client who had grown up in a situation where his single mother had become involved with a married man by whom she had given birth to my client. The affair, along with the child, was kept secret and not made known to the man's wife or his other children. My client shared how he had felt like an outsider all of his life as a result of knowing about his father's wife and children, but being kept separate from the "real family". He admitted that he grew up feeling like a dirty secret and was even referred to as a "bastard". Fast forward to the present when this client was struggling with feeling separate from God, and once again, felt like a "bastard". I suggested to him that he had been defining himself this way his entire life, and because he felt like an outcast from his father's family, he had projected those same feelings onto God and internalized them within himself. Once he was able to make the connection that he had been carrying this deep sense of shame and unworthiness as the result of his upbringing, he was able to accept that the circumstances surrounding his conception and birth were truly no fault of his own, and he was able to overcome lifelong feelings of rejection and exclusion.

Having a seat at the table is about our basic self-concept and understanding of who we are, what we are worth and knowing that our presence is meant to be seen, heard and felt. Deserving a seat at the table may be about belonging and inclusion, or it may be about understanding and accepting that we have certain rights. According to the constitution of the United States, American citizens have certain inalienable rights that give us the right to vote, the right to free speech, the right to fair housing, the right to worship without persecution, the right to an education and even the right to pursue the American dream. Our citizenship provides us these rights regardless of our gender, beliefs, income, relationship status, opinions, and any other number of characteristics. For those who were born in America, these rights are automatic at birth, while those from other countries are able to apply for and obtain citizenship. Having a seat at the table can also be granted by an employer and because of our position within the company, we are allowed to make certain decisions regarding the company. Our membership within clubs and organizations grant us access to certain rights and privileges. We also have rights within our marriages and as parents, we can help make decisions pertaining to our children.

While our inclusion in certain groups, organizations, relationships or positions can entitle us to have a seat at the table; there may be times when we have to demand and even fight for our seat at the table. Women in America fought and gained the right to vote in 1920 and are still fighting today for pay and gender equality. African-Americans have fought for a seat at the table from gaining freedom from slavery to earning voting rights, and we continue to fight for social justice and economic and racial equality. Simply because we deserve a seat at the table or we are entitled to one by our birthright, citizenship, or other levels of inclusion, does not automatically guarantee us a seat; therefore, sometimes we must be willing to face rejection, endure hardships and remain steadfast in our resolve either until our seat at the table is granted or we decide to create our own table. This is exactly what Tyler Perry did when he opened his own movie studio after being turned down by Hollywood. Because of his decision to create his own table, he has become the first Black man in America to own his own major motion picture studio. While this is an admirable achievement for him, it also opens the door and paves the way for others to follow his example. Fortunately, we now live in a time where we can build our own table, create our own platform, and level the playing field when our seat at the table is not readily granted or easily accessible.

Having a seat at the table is having a basic understanding of our value and worth as human beings without guilt, shame, or obligation and knowing that we deserve to be present, considered and included. As in the case of my client, once he understood who he really was and released the label that no longer defined nor served him, he was able to restore his sense of belonging, improve his self-worth and create a new definition of himself. He is now living life on his own terms and admits he no longer waits or asks for permission to show up or level up because he now knows he deserves a seat at the table.

I have worked hard to redefine myself and claim my seat at the table - whatever table that may be. I own my own business, I invest in myself and in my dreams, and I am creating a legacy for my children whilst setting an example for others to follow. I intend for my children to know that they need not feel excluded or uninvited because someone does not grant them a seat at their table.

While it took King David to convince Mephibosheth he deserved a seat at the king's table, we may have to validate this within and for ourselves. Maybe you were born into an undesirable situation like my client, or for some other reason never felt a sense of belonging or inclusion. Now is your time to remove those labels and definitions and as Shirley Chisolm stated "Even if they won't give you a seat at their table, you can pull up a folding chair."

Personal Reflection:

1) Make a list of labels and definitions that are outdated or inaccurate.

2) Make a list of times you felt like you were excluded and did not belong. What would change if you knew you belonged without anyone else's consent or approval?

Chapter 28

No Elevation without Evolution

"The whole point of being alive is to evolve
into the complete person you were intended to be"
~~Oprah Winfrey

One of the most popular phrases in recent times is "Level Up". Leveling up essentially means going to a higher level of success in our lives, careers, relationships or in regards to our talent or skill. I too have dreams and goals of leveling up and expanding my territory, increasing my degree of influence, earning six to seven figures and utilizing my gifts and talents of speaking, writing, coaching, and training to inspire, encourage and motivate. Leveling up for me is going global. While my life has certainly seen lots of highs over the past three years, I realize that I cannot fully reach my peak of elevation without the corresponding growth and evolution. I now understand why I had to go through certain things during this season such as letting go of people, redefining how I see myself and feel about myself, releasing my past, forgiving everyone including me, making peace with myself on all levels and fully accepting me, flaws and all. I could not understand or appreciate any of this as I was going through these trials and tribulations; instead I felt angry, defensive, depressed, alone, and afraid. I felt victimized and it truly seemed as if life, God, the universe and everyone in it were against me. I withdrew. I isolated myself. I hid. I laugh as I reflect on how life would not even allow me to do that, because while inwardly I was going through my own private hell, outwardly my life continued to be blessed. I started receiving more higher paying speaking engagements; my book sales were good and I was a featured author at the 2018 and 2019 Essence Festival with the top-rated talk radio show in my local area. People were starting to recognize me in public. All around me, my family and friends were congratulating me on my success and I remember people would comment on how God was blessing me and opening doors for me. I would smile graciously and say thank you while thinking to myself, "If they only knew". If they only knew all the insecurities I was had to face, fears that were coming up on a daily basis, past memories that were resurfacing, and even the anxiety and heart palpitations that became so bad I had to get a prescription for them. People were celebrating my elevation without knowing the first thing about my evolution. I realize now that it was necessary. It was necessary because I would never be able to handle what God was doing in my life while holding onto things, people, habits, beliefs and ideas that no longer served me. While I may have felt that life, God and the universe were punishing me, I understand now that it was all preparing me, pruning me and refining me. My old ways of thinking and being could not go into this new season with me. I would have sabotaged it (and did on several occasions), I would have tried to take along people who could not and were not meant to go, and I would have held on to the attitudes and beliefs that kept me believing who I was rather than redefining and accepting who I am. I also had to evolve into the woman who could accept and receive the things that God was doing in my life. I had to overcome my fears of stepping out and being seen, I had to overcome people-pleasing and I had to overcome my need for external validation, approval and affirmation. I had to address and resolve the trifecta of guilt, shame and blame. I had to forgive myself on every level and I had to forgive others no matter who and no matter what. I had to create a new relationship with myself and other people. I went from seeing people as enemies to seeing them as teachers with lessons that were helping me become my best version of myself. I had to give myself permission to rise above the image and concept I had of myself based on my past experiences and transform into someone who was worthy and deserving of the absolute best that life had to offer. I even had to change my relationship with money and increase my capacity to receive the amount of money I was envisioning for myself. So many people talk about leveling up and don't even realize they may not be ready and prepared to handle life on those levels. What I did not want to happen to me was what happened when I first learned about The Secret and The Law of Attraction fifteen years prior. I had gained the knowledge, insight, tools and techniques and I became great at manifesting and attracting the things I wanted, but because the woman on the inside of me was not able to handle those things, I slowly and systematically, sabotaged myself and lost everything I had built. I did not do this consciously or even knowingly, and if you had asked me, I would have blamed it on the economy, the housing market crash in 2008, or some other external culprit, but in reality, the poor little Black girl could not conceive or receive what was happening to me.

T. Harv Eker, author of The Millionaire Mind, says that each of us has a financial thermostat that works the same way as the thermostats in our homes. If the temperature in the home goes above what is set, the thermostat kicks on and brings it back down. If the temperature falls below the set point, the thermostat kicks on and raises it. Our financial thermostats and set points are based on our life experiences and our internal beliefs about money and wealth, and if we never raise our financial setpoints, then no matter how much we accomplish, earn and obtain, we will find a way to go back to our original setpoint. This explains why lottery winners end up broke in a few years; they received a blessing beyond what they could conceive or receive, and because their financial setpoints were set much lower, they subconsciously created circumstances to bring them back into balance with their internal beliefs. Sadly, because most of us are unaware of our real power, we blame outside circumstances, much like I did. Perhaps what was worse for me was that I knew the truth, but refused to accept responsibility for allowing my fears to overwhelm me and cause me to destroy what I had created. Even though I made a promise to myself to never allow it to happen again, truthfully, I still had not bought in 100% to the knowledge that I would have to shift my internal beliefs and raise my financial setpoint so that I would be able to maintain the things I wanted to attract and receive.

"No elevation without evolution" holds so much meaning for me now and I am grateful that God did not elevate me beyond what I could handle. I am now working to become the woman who can handle, manage and master the opportunities flowing into my life without waiting for the other shoe to drop, because inwardly I feel undeserving of my blessings. I have come to understand that when our blessings come in too quickly or too bountifully, it can feel like we are caught in a flood and if we are not feeling solid and stable, the flood waters can and will overtake us and make us feel as if we are drowning. Recently, I shared with a friend who would comment "Another blessing" on every social media post that I shared about some new achievement or opportunity. I told her how I would inwardly cringe every time I read her comment. When she asked why, I told her that my inner me believed I was receiving too many blessings and thought surely something bad would happen to destroy all of it. After hearing a message from Bishop T.D. Jakes that said God has an Eden for all of us which means that we can go from blessing to blessing and we do not have to experience calamity and catastrophe as a result. I realize that God desires to bless us and He desires for us to prosper and be in good health.

One of my favorite scriptures is Isaiah 54:2, "Enlarge the location of your tent, let the curtains of your dwellings be stretched wide, and don't hold back. Lengthen your cords; and strengthen your stakes." I now understand that we must prepare for what we are asking for by increasing and enlarging our ability and capacity to receive. As a result of me enlarging my own capacity, I no longer experienced overwhelming fear and anxiety when blessings came my way and I was able to receive without my insecurities rising to the surface to warn me to remind me of what I did not deserve. I can now openly and freely receive "another blessing".

As you consider the things you want to do and have in life, make sure you also consider the person you will need to be in order to receive those things. I urge you not to try and level up beyond your capacity to receive and manage life on that level. Do your inner work and raise your emotional, mental, relational, financial and success setpoints, so that when the flood of blessings comes, it does not overtake you.

Personal Reflection:

1) What is your current capacity to receive?

2) Is it in alignment with what you envision for your life?

Chapter 29

The Waiting Room

"The distance between your faith and
your arrival is the waiting room"
~~Pastor John Gray

As I was nearing the completion of this book, I got to a point where I began feeling extremely restless and frustrated. I had been married for eight years, I had been in private practice for eight years, and yet I felt no closer to achieving the big dreams I had, than when I started. At least, that was the way it appeared to me.

We were still living in the same home I had purchased as a real estate investment back in 2006, an while my husband had purchased a new car for me, our other two cars had declined significantly and it seemed like one or both of them were always in need of some repair. What's worse is that these are the same two vehicles my husband had been driving to work for the past eight years. He wanted a new truck. He deserved a brand-new truck. We needed a new home as we had outgrown our current one. As I calculated the years of financial commitments and the time and energy we had invested along with the years of tithing, sowing and believing for our next level, I became angry, restless and frustrated and I began to ask the question "When?".

Not only had my husband and I been doing the work externally, but we had also been doing the work internally. I had gone to therapy to address my past and I had watched countless motivational videos and purchased various courses. I had spent time alone with God seeking, asking, and praying. I had resolved several things and changed many of my limiting beliefs to empowering beliefs. I journaled. I read numerous accounts of other people's breakthroughs including Tyler Perry, Lizzo, and Tony Robbins. I watched movies about musical artists getting their first big break, (*The Temptations* was my favorite), and yet none of this seemed to be happening for us, me. I was told to be patient. Anyone who really knew me, knew I was impatient, highly energetic, headstrong, and that being patient was like kryptonite to Superman. I sucked at it. I came from a family of impatient people. In fact, I equated patience with laziness and a lack of ambition and motivation. Many of the patient people I knew were also procrastinators and I definitely did not want to be one of them. I had goals and dreams and I was determined to make it, not just for me, but for my family. I knew my husband was sacrificing his dream vehicle for me. I had quit my job to start my business, and then I had spent the past eight years working to make my business successful and lucrative. While I made a profit each year, I was nowhere close to the "riches" I had envisioned. I had financial goals and a business and marketing plan, but yet every year, I barely managed to stay in the positive. Thank God for my husband's devotion to me and my vision; however, we were both becoming impatient. We were both feeling the impact of being in a home we had outgrown. We both had big dreams and visions for our children and our family. Why then, hadn't it happened? Our big break. My big break. I began to question whether I had "it". It being the X-factor. That thing that separates artists from artists with Grammy award winning songs; actors from actors with Emmy awards; and athletes from Heisman trophy winners and MVPs. I compared myself to some of the people around me and what I saw was that I was just as educated, qualified, capable and hungry. People regularly told me I was on my way, my time was coming, and I was destined for greatness. Honestly, I had believed this since I was a kid. So, if I was destined to be great and I had been doing the work, then why had it not happened?

Finally, I had had enough and I literally told the universe, "I quit! Maybe I am not supposed to be this great celebrity life coach, therapist and international speaker that I envisioned myself being.

186

Maybe I really do not have "it" and the past eight years of effort and investment have all been wasted." I threw a temper tantrum of epic proportions as I wondered aloud, "Why not me?! When is it going to be my turn?!" While I had experienced some level of success, the big win was yet to show up. When I finally calmed down and started seeking God for understanding, I began to ask myself, "What is God trying to teach me in this waiting season?"

I was very familiar with the concept of seasons, but this waiting season I was in felt different. It wasn't a season of movement or transition or elevation, this was a season of what felt like dormancy and inactivity. I read once that in nature, the winter season is described as the season where nothing is growing or blooming, but this is also when plants store up enough energy for the new growth they will experience in the Spring. I realized that my waiting season was as necessary for my growth, evolution and elevation as any other season. It was true that I had been doing the work, both internally and externally. Like a farmer planting crops, I had been sowing my seeds during those years through my financial investment, hard work, perseverance and resilience. I had also undergone a pruning season where I had released and let go of things, habits, beliefs, and even people that no longer served my highest purpose. Now I was in a season that appeared dormant and as if nothing was happening. It was then that I realized I could either wait and be angry, impatient, and frustrated, or I could just wait. I could wait and trust that my seeds were in good ground and would produce a harvest in due time. I could wait and trust that God and I had pruned off the dead things, allowing for my maximum growth potential. So, I released my anger and frustration and decided I would wait with expectancy and I would learn to trust the process of life unfolding. I knew I had already grown and learned so much; surely, I would not give up now, not just before my seeds broke ground.

The morning after my meltdown, my best friend sent me a text that described how airplanes are sometimes unable to land because of unfavorable ground conditions and therefore have to remain in the air circling the landing strip until it is safe enough to land. This is known as a holding pattern. Because this happens on a regular basis, planes are always equipped with extra fuel to be able to remain airborne until the control tower gives clearance that it is okay to land. That was exactly how I had been feeling…like I was going around in circles, waiting for my breakthrough that had not yet happened. As I reflected on the purpose of a holding pattern, I began to understand that God wasn't just holding me back or delaying my success, He was actually using this season of waiting as preparation. He was literally making sure the conditions were favorable and safe enough for me to land. I then decided that if I was going to have to wait, then I needed to learn how. I intentionally started studying waiting seasons and how to navigate the meantime. I repeatedly listened to a gospel song by Juanita Bynum called "I Don't Mind Waiting" where she was not only singing about waiting, but she was actually saying it was a privilege and an honor to wait. All of a sudden, there was the epiphany! If I was waiting on God, then my waiting actually meant that I had a belief and a promise that He was coming! I thought about how I had never before waited on something that I hadn't asked for, ordered, or requested. In fact, the very act of asking for something initiates the process of expecting and waiting for its delivery. As one of Amazon's most faithful customers and a member of Prime, I know that when I order something, I will be given an expected delivery date. Even more so, since I signed up for text alerts through the app, I also get a message telling me when my order ships, what day it's expected to arrive and even how many stops away my order is on a map. Not once have I expected not to receive what I ordered even though there have been one or two times something was delayed. However, because I fully expect that Amazon will either refund me or make the necessary arrangements to get it to me, I do not become angry, impatient or upset. So, although my breakthrough had not yet arrived in the manner I was anticipating, I knew I had to trust God's divine timing, which is way more reliable than Amazon!

Just as in a human pregnancy, there is a gestational period that takes place before the actual birth; the spiritual Law of Gestation states that for every seed, there is a set gestation or incubation period that particular seed needs in order be established and manifest into its physical form. Our responsibility is to learn to honor and respect this divinely orchestrated process. When we become impatient, which is a form of resistance, we actually delay the process and cause it to take longer.

The Bible calls patience a virtue and describes patience as vital, because it helps us to trust in the goodness of God and to have faith that He will keep His word and do what He promised. Even though my seeds had not all materialized, was I honoring and respecting the Law of Gestation? Did I have faith that God would come through for me and my family? I knew God had already come through in numerous situations in the past and that we had never missed a meal or been late on a payment. What we had done was grow closer as a family and learn how to make a lot from a little while having a great time in the process.

Transitions

In addition to learning the importance of waiting, I about transitions. A quote by an unknown author stated "Your life is a story of transition. You are always leaving one chapter behind for the next."

It was 2018 and I had just produced my first women's empowerment event, The Breathe Women's Conference, and it was a huge success. We had great attendance, plenty of food, the program flowed well and everyone seemed to have an amazing time. For the next few days, I was on cloud nine. Then it happened. About a week after my event, I crashed and burned. I wasn't just physically and mentally exhausted as was to be expected, this was something more. Something deeper. I cried. I was irritable and I withdrew from everyone except my husband and children. I refused to get on social media to post or celebrate the success of my event. There were days when I did not even have my phone near me or remember where I left it because I had so disconnected from anything outside of my house and my office. To make matters worse, I had no idea what was wrong with me. I had heard from a friend that she went through a similar thing after her women's event and I wondered about the connection and the meaning of it. Finally, having no answers, I began to seek God and I went within. It was a few days when I received the revelation that "You can't live between seasons. You can't move forward into the next season and keep one foot behind in the former season. You have to be willing to completely release the former, so you can fully enter and embrace the new". All of a sudden, I saw an image of myself sitting on a fence and I understood. My inner conflict was the result of my old self not wanting to enter my new season. The wounded self that I had become familiar with for much of my adult life; the fearful me, the angry me, the me with low self-esteem, the people-pleaser and the approval seeker was still tethered to my old season of pain and struggle, and she was unable to enter this next level season of blessing. She was tied to the familiar, the past, and our previous limitations. What I discovered was that we cannot fully inhabit two seasons or two opposing spaces at the same time. I had been working for and striving to reach my next level season, but I had not fully released the comfort, safety, and familiarity of my current/former season. I then began to understand that this in between stage that was filled with discomfort, unrest, pain, sadness, darkness and isolation was actually a part of the transition process itself. Much like a caterpillar undergoing metamorphosis, I too was undergoing a period of great transformation in my growth and healing. It also reminded me of when the children of Israel left Egypt on their way to Canaan only to become stuck in the wilderness. The Bible says it was an 11-day journey that took them 40 years. I knew that it was going to be up to me as far as how long this transition period lasted and how intense it would get. I began to pray, fast, seek, study and read. I listened to motivational messages. I did acupressure tapping. I meditated. I journaled. The holidays came and while I enjoyed myself overall, deep down I was still struggling. What was worse is that I could not even discuss it with my friends and my husband, because I felt no one would completely understand it. I felt like I was in a cocoon. I was alone, in the darkness, isolated, uncertain and afraid. In the book, *The Game of Life and How to Play It*, author Florence Scovell Shinn shares a story of one of her students asking how long we must remain in the dark. Her response was, "Until you can see in the dark". It was in the darkness that I started to gain clarity, insight and understanding of seasons and transitions. I discovered that while the cocoon was dark, scary and isolated, it was also the way through to the next stage just as the wilderness was the way through to the Promised Land for the Israelites, and the cocoon is the way through for the caterpillar. This insect that used to push itself along on the ground to get from place to place bursts forth as a new creation, barely recognizable to itself.

I recently shared with a friend how my life is becoming unrecognizable to me because when I look back over all that I have been through and all that I have been through; then I look at where I am and see the vision of where I am going; it is almost as if it is happening to someone else, but in reality it is happening to me. Actually, it is happening in me and through me.

If you are going through your own period of transition, transformation and change from one season to the next, you will have to let go of one so you can fully inhabit the other. Be willing to remain in the darkness, face the unknown and the unfamiliar so that like the butterfly, you too will emerge as a new creation that is barely recognizable even to yourself.

Embracing Change

One of the hardest things in life for us to accept is change. I once read that change is the only thing that is constant and when I think about it, I must agree. My life has been full of changes and until very recently. I resisted change with everything I had in me. For me, change was scary. Change was unpredictable. At times, change was random. It came without warning or notice. Change required things that I had not yet mastered in life such as trusting the process, believing in myself and feeling safe and secure in the midst of transition. From animals and plants to the solar system and humans, everything is in motion and everything is ever changing. Seasons change, relationships change, time changes, technology changes, and the weather changes. In the human body, our cells literally regenerate on a daily basis, so it's not just that we are not the same as we were five years ago, we are not the same as we were one day ago. Everything and everyone change. I have learned that change is a part of life and perhaps change is life steadily unfolding and moving forward. When I think of how I and so many other people around the word resist and fear change, it seems a bit irrational and illogical because if nothing changed, things would cease to grow, and everything and everyone would eventually die. If nothing changed, babies would remain babies and never experience the joys of learning to walk and talk or growing up and getting older. The bottom line is, "to resist change is to resist life and the process of living itself." When I really began to examine my life, I could see how detrimental resisting change had been to my emotional and mental development. Being resistant to change has caused me to fear leaving my comfort zone and to continue to play it safe. Resisting change has caused me to hold on to things way longer than I should even if those things were doing me more harm than good. Resisting change has caused me to stay in unhealthy relationships, unfulfilling jobs and other unpleasant situations. I have come to accept that because change is a natural process and part of life, we can choose to get to a place where we no longer fear change and actually begin to embrace it. This requires a certain level of trust and faith that no matter what, we will be okay. Perhaps, this is the underlying reason why we fear change. Maybe, deep down, we fear that we will not be okay and that things may not work out in our favor; therefore, we hold on, hold back, stand down, stay quiet, resist, refuse, and reject many of the opportunities that life offers us to change and grow. Conversely, there are times in life when we may be eager for things to change. Times when life isn't going the way we planned it and times when we are in emotional or physical pain. I can recall wanting nothing more than for things to change so I could stop hurting after the loss of my mother. Likewise, anyone struggling through a tough season in life such as a divorce or illness can attest that they are longing for things to change and get better. Clients I work with that are suffering from depression, panic attacks, mood swings or suicidal thoughts are actually desperate for things to change and have their situations turn around. The reality is that whether we become comfortable with changes in our lives or not, we will not be able to escape or avoid change and the more we resist it, the harder life becomes. Again, I think it's the fear of the unknown and what we think the change will bring about that scares us most, along with the uncertainty of whether we will come out of it okay. This goes back to the concept of control that I spoke about in a previous chapter. The tighter we try and hold onto the reins, the more resistant we are to the natural flow of life and the more we will experience the pressure and the consequences of swimming against the current and paddling upstream.

In reality, we were not created or born to resist change. In fact, the process of birth itself is the very definition of change and transformation. From conception through gestation and birth, we undergo a multitude of changes, many of which would cause catastrophic issues and birth defects were they not to occur. Once we are born, we continue to go through major changes just in the first year of life such as walking, sitting up, and speaking our first words. From that first year to starting school, we undergo changes in our fine and gross motor skills that allow us to run and skip and play and count and recite our ABC's. The point is, we were meant to grow and evolve, and the more we can learn to embrace and accept that, the easier life becomes. I often advise my clients to become comfortable being uncomfortable, which greatly helps us when we are seeking to begin or change careers, write a book, or start a business. There will always be a period of time when we will experience the discomfort that comes from the uncertain, the unpredictable, and the unknown. We all can think of times when we went through a change that we initially feared or resisted, only to discover that it was not as bad as we thought it would be and ended up working out for the best. If we can keep in mind that life is on our side, even in the rough times, and continue to affirm that all things work together for our good, then it can make the process of change easier.

We have only to pay attention to nature to understand that it does not resist change. Summer does not resist the coming of Fall, nor does Fall resist the coming of Winter. Perhaps everything other than you and I seems to instinctively know and accept change as a natural part of its growth and evolution, and since we now know that change is the only constant there is, we can make the decision to reduce our own resistance to change and maybe even learn to embrace it.

As I complete this chapter, my family is in the midst of building a beautiful, new home and my husband has a new job fifteen minutes away. We continue to sow faithfully and expectantly, trusting and believing that God will deliver as promised and that our waiting rooms and holding patterns are preparation for our landing.

Personal Reflection:

1) Are you stuck between the old version of yourself and who you are becoming?

2) How can you ease the distress of transitioning from one season to the next?

3) Where are you afraid of, or resisting change in your life?

4) What would happen if you surrender and embrace the changes?

Chapter 30

What Defines You?

"What defines you ultimately determines your destiny"
~~Giovanna Geathers

In 2015, I was asked to serve as keynote speaker at the Savannah State University women's conference. The title of my presentation was "What Defines You?" I shared this information for the second time at my women's retreat and even developed a quote: "Whatever defines you also determines your destiny". As I have come to understand the importance of knowing what defines us, I can say with confidence that it does determine what we do, how we do it, where we go, if we go and how far we go. To define something or someone is to give meaning to it and to identify and determine the essential qualities of it, including its nature, capabilities, functionality, characteristics, design, performance and even its flaws and limitations. It becomes how we identify it and also influences our expectations of it. Cellphones are defined as electronic devices that make and receive calls, send text messages, give us internet access, take pictures and videos, and keep track of our calendars. The definition of the cell phone gives us its identity and defines and determines what it can and what it cannot do. The original cellphone had a large bulky design and could only be used in the car so it was called a "mobile phone". Now cellphones are so small they fit in our pockets and can go almost anywhere. The original cell phones did not have cameras in them and they were not defined as "smartphones". Our current cellphones now come with mobile applications that can assist us in a variety of ways well beyond the cellphone's original design and use. The cellphone has evolved and based on recent advertising; cellphones will soon have the capability to do so much more than we ever imagined. But, despite the fact that cellphones have evolved significantly, the reality is they are still limited. For example, our cellphones cannot drive us to work, tuck our children into bed at night or comfort a loved one who is going through a difficult time. The cellphone's definition determines its usage, identity, description and its limitations. This is true for every other thing on the planet, i.e. bodies of water are defined as rivers, streams, oceans, or swamps.

As human beings, we have also learned to define ourselves. We define ourselves by gender, culture, ethnicity, language, age, education, socioeconomic status, sexual orientation, relationship status, skill level, talents and gifts. People are also defined by height, weight, stature, skin tone, hair color, eye color, etc. We are defined by our religious and spiritual beliefs, political beliefs, and other topics of social and human interest. We can define ourselves by our experiences, parents, peers, schools, abilities, disabilities, social network, peer groups, and geographic location. And we can define ourselves by our adverse life experiences which shape our attitudes, beliefs, thoughts, behaviors and ideas about ourselves and others, and become the labels we assign to ourselves which have a direct and an indirect impact on our self-image, self-worth, and self-esteem. Sadly, many people are still being held back and controlled by the definitions and the labels that have been placed on them by others. As a psychotherapist, I often see the deleterious effects of this on people who may have been defined in negative ways and terms. People who have been defined as stupid, worthless, inadequate, lacking, broken, defective, and unwanted often struggle to overcome the impact of these labels and definitions. Children who are labeled in school as troublemakers or problem children often continue to display and exhibit troublesome problematic behaviors throughout their lives. Children labeled as learning disabled, emotionally handicapped and developmentally delayed may end up fulfilling the expectations that go along with those labels and never outgrow them.

It was while writing this chapter that life taught me an immeasurable lesson in redefining myself. I was at a luncheon for a women's conference and a young lady mentioned to me that she was writing a book and she asked me, "Do you know how when you're writing a book about your life, you start living the chapters?" I was stunned as I wondered how she could have possibly known that what she said was my exact experience. The truth is I had been experiencing epiphany after epiphany and revelation after revelation throughout this process, so even though I wanted to simply write this book and share my experiences objectively, life required that I learn and apply these concepts subjectively. Sometimes I laugh when I think about how amazing life is in making sure we walk the walk and not just talk the talk.

Writing this chapter of Epiphany has taught me just how deep the definitions of other people have gone in my life. I was being defined by my culture, my community, my gender, my background, my upbringing, my abuse, my family, and people's perceptions of me from the moment I was born. These definitions have been controlling and influencing me my entire life. They have caused me to see myself in unsupportive ways. They caused me to think and present myself as someone who was unworthy, undeserving, inadequate, inferior, poor, abused, unattractive, not smart enough, and not good enough. Things that had been spoken to me and over me throughout my life had helped shape my own image of myself. Other people's ideas, opinions, perceptions and beliefs became my ideas, opinions, perceptions and beliefs about me and the world around me. I viewed middle class and rich people a certain way. I viewed people who were different from me in certain ways. It literally wasn't until I started writing this chapter that I recognized and admitted to myself that many of my current thoughts, opinions, ideas and beliefs were not even mine. I realized that I had allowed past experiences to tell me who I was, who I wasn't, what I was and what I wasn't, in addition to what I was allowed to do, be and have and what was not ok for me to do, be and have. I saw myself as the same poor little Black girl who grew up in a small town in the South and I told myself certain things based on that perception, concept and image of me. I thought about my family's dysfunction: drug use, alcoholism, sexual abuse, incarceration, and poverty, and I realized that somewhere along the journey of my life I had decided that those labels also fit me, although I had never experienced all of them. Because of how my family was seen and perceived by others in our community, I unconsciously decided it must be true of me also. I see this same phenomenon in families who struggle with various generational curses, habits and proclivities from gambling to promiscuity to certain illnesses and diseases. I often hear people claim them by saying "Cancer runs in my family" or All the men in our family die of heart attacks before age 60". Unknowingly, people have subconsciously adopted those same beliefs about themselves, and many will end up developing the same curses, habits, illnesses and addictions. When I began to fully understand that I not only needed to redefine how I saw myself from inside out, and not just work towards making sure the outside appeared a certain way, it literally set me free to become everything I have ever wanted to be. I intentionally started to think about how I saw me, flaws and all. I wrote a list of those negative things and then went through it asking and answering honestly as to whether it was really my belief, thought and idea or one I had taken on from someone else. Through this process, I have come to discover what true authenticity really means. It is not just the idea of speaking your truth or telling that truth to others. It is more than being willing to be vulnerable and transparent. Real authenticity requires us to be real with ourselves first. It requires that we do the work to discover, get to know and fully accept ourselves unconditionally. It is the courage and the willingness to define or redefine yourself and your life on your own terms in the present, regardless of your past failures, mistakes, habits, insecurities and predispositions. It is examining your life and releasing what is not authentically you, but what you took on by default of your family, culture, race, gender, upbringing, or life experiences.

I realized that I had to create a healthier image of me because otherwise I would never be able to fully accept and receive everything that life has for me. I would never go to the heights, depths and levels that God desires for me because the old me would have sabotaged it, as it had for many years. Suddenly, I understood why I would always get right to the finish line of some new idea or business venture and fail to cross over. A part of me did not see me as a finisher. A part of me could not see me as a winner. A part of me still saw me as broken, inadequate and incomplete. How could I become a millionaire when I had grown up in poverty? How could I step out and do something amazing and monumental when I came from a family of limiting beliefs? How could I help change and transform the world when I was a survivor of sexual abuse? I discovered that living free really means deciding for yourself who you are and living that truth despite circumstances and evidence to the contrary. It means knowing what you are worth, knowing what you deserve and asking for it, demanding it and moving towards it without apologizing, minimizing, explaining and rationalizing any gift, talent, ability, or blessing.

During this same time in my life, my former sister-in-law reached out to me to perform a dramatic monologue at her church's Black History month program. Initially, I declined the invitation. I even laughed as I told myself that I hadn't performed in years and had too much going on in the present to memorize and perform a poem. Then I thought about it and admitted that I really had a fear of people saying, "What is she doing now? She is already writing books, speaking, planning women's conferences and retreats, running a practice, and raising two young children". When I admitted to myself what was really holding me back, I immediately messaged her and asked for another opportunity. I studied all week and that Sunday; I delivered my performance with laser-like precision. I did not do it for recognition or to be seen or applauded. I did it to be true to me and to redefine who I say I am. I did it to demonstrate to myself that I am willing and ready to own all of my gifts and talents, and I owe no one an apology for being me. All my life I have been told I was either too little or too much and for years I have denied, avoided, minimized, and hidden my gifts in fear of rejection, criticism, judgment or abandonment by other people. Guess what? People have still rejected me, criticized me, judged me, and left me. The truth is that no matter who we are and no matter what we do, we are never going to please everyone and continuing to define ourselves by other people's ideas and opinions keeps us enslaved and imprisoned. We will never rise above the images we have in our minds, and if we are defining ourselves in negative or limited ways because of past mistakes, experiences and other people, then we will never rise to our full potential and live our lives with boldness and authenticity. Yes, we can consider other people's opinions as there is wisdom and maturity in being able to listen and learn, but we do not have to automatically agree if it does not truly serve where we are in the present and where we see ourselves in the future. Redefining ourselves does not mean pretending our past doesn't exist, or that certain things have not happened. It means committing ourselves to live and define who we are NOW.

Someone once asked me how I became so confident and I laughed because confidence is still a work in progress for me. What I said to her was that I decided who I wanted to become and I became her. Actually, I am continually becoming her daily as I open myself up to new ideas, beliefs, changes and experiences. The woman I am today looks very different from the woman I was ten years or even six months ago, and the woman I am becoming tomorrow will look different from the woman I am today. The truth is that I now define myself based on the beliefs, ideas, knowledge and wisdom that better serves who I choose to be. While that old, small version of me is still there, she is not as afraid anymore of who we are becoming. When I think about it, it seems that as soon as I become confident in leaping from one level, life says, now come up to this higher level and leap from here. My job, and yours, is to trust the process and jump

Personal Reflection:

1) In what ways have you allowed past memories and experiences to define who you are?

2) In what ways have you allowed other people to define who you are?

3) How would redefining yourself serve you now?

Chapter 31

Entanglements

"You'll learn, as you get older, that rules are made to be broken. Be bold enough to live life on your terms, and never, ever apologize for it."
~~Mandy Hale

As I write this chapter, I am reflecting on how many times in my life I have willingly followed written and unwritten, spoken and unspoken, expressed and implied rules. There were rules to follow for my gender, my family, my church, my school, and even my race as an African-American. Even though following the rules may have kept me safe and protected in some ways, it kept me trapped in many others. In fact, following the rules was the very thing that was keeping me from being truly happy and reaching my ultimate potential.

It wasn't until I was working in my private practice that I became keenly aware of the rules we follow that prevent us from living our best lives. What I discovered was that these rules, which I call vows, covenants and agreements are often imposed upon us by others and can become so indoctrinated in us that they literally hold us back, sabotage our potential and keep us in bondage out of fear of breaking or going against them. While these vows, covenants and agreements can be unspoken and unwritten, many times we readily accept them as factual, actual, and true, and because of that, they become mentally, emotionally, spiritually, physically, and financially binding.

By definition, an agreement is a binding arrangement between two or more parties. It is also defined as consent, approval and being of the same opinion with the parties with which you are in agreement. For example, two business owners may create a legal partnership that has certain legal restrictions and penalties if the agreement is broken. Again, these agreements are often unspoken, yet incredibly powerful in influencing our thoughts, feelings and behaviors.

A vow is defined as a promise or set of promises that commits us to a particular role or course of action. Marriage is a great example, in that a couple commits to keeping the vows of the marriage agreement and must go through legal means to dissolve the marriage and break their vows.

A covenant is defined as a contract and a binding promise between individuals, groups, or nations and contains social, legal, religious, and financial aspects, i.e. peace treaties between countries, marriages, and mortgage loans. It is important for us to understand the unspoken vows, covenants and agreements we may be adhering to because they have the power to define us and determine our course of action in life. For example, if no one in a particular family ever graduates from high school, then someone with an intention to graduate may be looked upon as breaking a family agreement which can have serious repercussions.

One of the main things I hear from people who admit to being afraid to pursue their dreams is the fear of what people will think, and often the people with the most influence over us are our family members. What is interesting is that these vows, covenants and agreements may be passed down from generation to generation without anyone ever questioning or examining them to see if they truly line up with our own personal beliefs and opinions. Many times, we just accept them as the way things are supposed to be done.

There is a story Zig Ziglar tells about a newly married woman whose husband asked her why she cut the ends off the ham when cooking it. The woman replied that her mother had always done it that way so she believed that was the way it was supposed to be. The husband then calls his mother-in-law to ask her the same question and learns that her own mother had always cut the ends off the ham which was why she did it that way. When the husband called the grandmother, he discovered that the reason she had always cut the ends off the ham was because she had a small oven and cutting off the ends was the only way it would fit. This is a great example of how things are accepted, passed down, and perpetuated over and over again without question or examination.

As I examined my own life, I realized that I too had been holding onto some vows, covenants and agreements that were causing me to hold back and play small, out of fear of outshining my friends and family. I knew they were proud of me and I believed they were genuinely happy for me, but somewhere deep inside of me, I felt I was stepping away from the group and breaking a rule. I had grown up feeling as if I was constantly being compared to my younger sister who I felt was my mother's favorite. I spent a lot of my time trying to earn my mother's approval and praise only to have it downplayed when compared with some wonderful new thing my sister had done. While I am uncertain as to why this happened, the story I told myself was that my sister was always supposed to outdo me. Thankfully it never damaged my relationship with her, but honestly, I struggled with feelings of guilt and fear whenever I appeared to be breaking the rules and "outdoing" my sister. The crazy thing is that I never set out to outdo anyone and was only ever doing what came naturally to me, but still I held back, almost apologetically, for fear of making anyone feel threatened or insecure around me. I realized that not only was I adhering to the unspoken vows, covenants and agreements within my family, but I had unintentionally created my own limiting beliefs that were "binding" me and keeping me from moving fully into my destiny.

During this time, a friend suggested I read the book by TD Jakes entitled, "Can You Stand to Be Blessed". The day after her suggestion, another friend sent me a video compilation that included TD Jakes speaking on this very subject. I listened as he shared that it takes courage to be blessed and live blessed because we will encounter jealousy, envy, and competition from other people. I now realize and accept that it does take courage to be blessed, to be set apart, to step out in faith, take a risk and pursue your destiny. Family members may shun you; friendships may end and relationships may shift. People who once cheered you on may now crucify you, and the group that you once felt such a part of and so in tune with may now ostracize, criticize, and reject you. This is when courage becomes essential; the courage to withstand the pressure in order to break free and become your own best version of yourself. As I reflected on my own entanglements, I made a solemn commitment to be willing to suffer the consequences, go against tradition and break the vows, covenants and agreements to which I had silently and unknowingly given consent. I gave myself permission to be great and to embody my greatness boldly and unapologetically. Not outdo or outshine anyone, but to be faithful to me and the God inside of me.

In addition to breaking my family and friendship vows, covenants and agreements, I also had to break the vows, covenants and agreements of being a Black woman both within my own community and the community at large. Sadly, I am all too familiar with how some of the unspoken agreements to "Keep it real and Keep it 100" as a race have prevented numerous African-Americans from stepping out, going against the grain and breaking the rules so they can live out their true purpose and potential in life.

When we become willing to acknowledge and identify the entanglements that are no longer serving who and where we are, we will be able to release their hold on us and reclaim our freedom and autonomy!

Personal Reflection:

1) Do you have any familial or relational vows, covenants or agreements that are no longer serving you and keeping you entangled?

2) How would your life be different if you had the courage to go against them and break free?

3) Do you have the courage it takes to be blessed and live blessed? If not, what can you begin doing today to boost your courage?

Chapter 32

Mommy Issues

"Love is the Divine Mother's arms,
when those arms are spread, every Soul falls into them"
~~Hazrat Inayat Khan

My mother died in February of 2016 at the age of 81 after a struggle with COPD and other age-related complications. She had smoked as a young woman, and although she quit many years ago, the damage to her lungs was irreversible and after a second bout with pneumonia, she was placed on oxygen for the duration of her time here on earth. Two weeks prior to her death, she phoned each of us and told us she would be transitioning soon. Each of us reacted to this in our own way. For me, it was surreal because my mother had always seemed invincible, like she could withstand and overcome any challenge she faced; so when her health began to decline and she started experiencing signs of dementia, it was shocking for me to watch this strong, formidable force of nature become fragile and almost childlike in the sense that there were many things she could no longer do for herself. During the weeks leading up to her death, my mother and I shared some very special moments together despite our decades-long strained relationship. One of those moments was when my mother shared her funeral arrangements with me. "Why me?" I wondered. I was the next to youngest child. She then told me that I was her strongest child and she knew I could handle it. I remember thinking to myself that my being strong wasn't because I wanted to be; it was because I had to be. Many times, I felt overlooked and disregarded by my family. Growing up in a family of seven, I felt like I was always trying to figure out where I fit. It seemed that my paternal grandmother favored my brothers; my youngest brother, who was what we would now call a special needs child, was not only favored by my grandmother, but also by my maternal aunt and my mother; my oldest sister was favored by my paternal aunt; and my baby sister seemed to clearly be my mother's favorite. That left me, "nobody's favorite". And since I had no idea why no one favored me, in my childlike thinking, I decided that it was because something was either missing in me or wrong with me. Unfortunately, this led to my continual search for ways to measure up and stand out and be seen and acknowledged. Because my mother and I always had such a strained relationship and would bump heads over the simplest things, I flat out felt my mother did not like me much of the time. Due to the fact that we derive so much of who we believe we are from our parents (and my father was not there to fill in the blanks), I went through much of my life not liking my own self. What I felt had been missing in my relationship with my mother, I sought externally in my romantic relationships with men, my friendships with women and even from my teachers, employers and other authority figures. I had no way of knowing the full impact of mine and my mother's relationship until the day before the fourth anniversary of her death. I had been going through yet another issue that had become all too familiar to me where another woman in my life, without warning, had stopped speaking to me for no apparent reason. If there had been reason, she had not been willing to share it with me. Because I was such a consummate people-pleaser, I tried my best to figure out what I had done wrong and how I could make up for it. Finally, I had had enough and I decided I was no longer going to allow other people to have this much effect on me. The very next day as I was praying and meditating, I felt God's presence come over me very strongly. This in and of itself wasn't alarming as I often felt the presence of God, but this time was different. As I lay in bed that morning, I began to feel God's presence shift from the masculine energy it had always been, to a very soft, ethereal, feminine energy. In essence, I saw an image of God as a woman reaching out to me with open arms, beckoning me to come to her. I was completely stunned as I allowed myself to be swept up and enveloped in this warm, loving, feminine embrace that I had never experienced before. While I was quite familiar with Bible verses about God being a mother to the motherless, I had never personally sought or experienced God as a mother. All of my images of Him were masculine and I had always thought of and referred to Him as father and daddy. I reflected back on the movie, *The Shack*, where God is portrayed as several different people including a Black woman. The reason this characterization of God in various forms stood out to me so much was because I had once heard Iyanla Vanzant speak of God becoming who and what we need during specific moments in our lives, so on that particular day, the day before the anniversary of my mother's passing, I experienced God as a powerful force of feminine energy, unlike anything I had ever felt or imagined. I cried as I surrendered myself to this overwhelming presence of divine love and acceptance. It was then that I heard my mother's voice speaking to me.

My mother, who had been the source of so much distress in my life and from whom I felt I had never gained approval and acceptance, was telling me that her inability to give me what I needed had absolutely nothing to do with me. I felt my heart soften as she lovingly assured me that it was not because I was broken, defective, damaged or inadequate. As she called me by my childhood nickname, "Vonnie", my mother said to me softly but firmly, "Vonnie, it wasn't because of you, it was because of me". She went on to tell me that the love, acceptance and approval I had been seeking in everyone and everything else was because of what I did not receive from her. She then validated me, gave me her approval and told me to go live the life I had been created to live without fear or apology. The last thing she said was that I no longer needed anyone else's permission to succeed, to be happy and to win.

My mother's confession and declaration of love that day caused decades of guilt, hurt, pain, anger, blame and shame to fall off of me in a matter of minutes! Instantly, I was liberated from years of false conclusions and wrong thinking about my mother, but more importantly, about myself. Instantly, I knew I was not damaged, inadequate, or guilty of anything and I no longer had to live my life in the mental and emotional prison within which I had been living. I wept, as a river of emotion rose up from the depths of my soul and left me feeling drained and empty, but also surprisingly light and free.

It was then that I understood why I had experienced so much pain and disappointment in my relationships with women and why I had never really trusted them. I understood why I have been called to help women heal and why my main platform involves women. I understand why it is so important for me to give my daughter the emotional love and support that she needs from me instead of having her seek it in everyone else. I also understand why God had to become a mother to me in those moments so I could release the pain I had been carrying inside of me for years. I was even able to understand why I had to have a hysterectomy to remove my womb. Like many other women, I had shut off and disconnected from my own femininity. I blamed it for making me weak and powerless, because I had never recognized its inherent strength and how necessary it is to our growth and development. I discovered that there is a spiritual Law of Gender that basically says there is masculine and feminine energy in everything and we need to nurture one as much as the other to truly live our lives in balance and harmony. Even our physical bodies carry both masculine and feminine hormones regardless of our gender. There are many women I have encountered throughout my life who have also struggled in their relationships with women and much of that is the result of our relationships with our mothers; if a father is the first man a girl falls in love with, then a mother is a woman's first best friend.

The presence of God that day as a mother was overwhelming, yet comforting and liberating as I felt myself begin to radiate from within and reclaim my feminine energy and power. It goes without saying that I completely forgave my mother that day and released all of pent-up pain and anguish which has gave me the freedom to begin reconnecting with women on a deeper level. Perhaps the greatest thing that came from that experience is that I am no longer angry and critical of the woman on the inside of me, and I have been able to make peace with her, embrace her and behold her true feminine power, beauty and strength.

Personal Reflection:

1. Are you a woman who tends to struggle in your relationships with other women? Do you or did you have a good relationship with your mother? If not, how has this affected you?

2. Are you a woman who has rejected or restricted your feminine energy? How does this show up in your life?

3. Have you ever been accused of being too aggressive or masculine?

Chapter 33

Integrity

"And you, you scare people because you are whole all by yourself"
~~Lauren Alex Hooper

When most of us think about the word integrity, we usually think of it in terms of honesty, doing the right thing, ethics, morals, sincerity, trustworthiness, and uprightness. This is also how I defined it. I pride myself on being a person of integrity in that I am loyal, honest, fair, and trustworthy, and I strive to be upright in my dealings with people; however, the first time I was introduced to the second definition of integrity was when my former pastor preached about it one Sunday and defined integrity as sound, stable, single-minded, and solid. He explained that integrity comes from the root word 'integer' which means whole and complete. I later discovered that the word "integrity" also means being our authentic selves no matter who we are in the company of; therefore, we do not have a "work self, home self, social self, or relationship self". We show up as the real us all the time, which is not always an easy thing to do when we are seeking external acceptance and approval. In those instances, we find ourselves changing and adapting to fit what we perceive other people or a situation requires of us. Most of the time this is the result of a past incident where we felt judged, rejected, criticized. for being our true selves and we responded by denying and concealing who we really were at our core. Some of us may even create false identities to show up in certain situations, i.e. the confident self that shows up at work but is insecure in interpersonal relationships. Perhaps it is in our relationships where we see this most. In my first book, I speak about how we often show up as our relationship representatives in the beginning of new relationships and while this may immediately sound deceptive, it could simply be that we have gotten so used to hiding who we really are that we often do not feel comfortable allowing someone else to see the real us until we get to know them and determine that they are safe and trustworthy.

As a psychotherapist, I often have clients who have been wounded at some point in their lives and have subconsciously created other selves and identities, not necessarily in what we once called multiple identity disorder - now referred to as Dissociative Identity Disorder (DID) - but in the sense that people often have "parts". Sometimes these parts are referred to as the inner child and over the past eight years in practice, I have found that most of us have parts. Whenever we are presented with a decision to make and we feel torn, this is an indication of two conflicting parts. There may be a part of us that wants to accept a job offer while another "part" of us feels uncertain. In people who have experienced trauma, there is typically solid evidence of parts, but not all parts develop due to trauma. I have seen the same phenomenon in people who grew up without abuse or neglect but felt their emotional needs were unmet. This could be due to a parent working out of town, a parent struggling with substance abuse or their own mental health issues, or parents who were physically present, but emotionally unavailable. It can happen with parents who were overly critical or had high expectations which caused their children to feel the need to be perfect or that they were never good enough. What happens is that the person may continue to grow physically and chronologically, but the little boy or girl inside of them stays frozen at a particular age or stage of life. These adult men and women then enter into relationships looking for someone else to meet and fulfill their unmet needs, or they may continually strive to overachieve in their educational and career goals to try and fill that void. One of my primary objectives is in helping people to become whole in and of themselves. I do this by working with the different parts and aspects of a person and integrating them into the whole self. As a result, the person often feels less divided, confused, conflicted, torn, fragmented and double-minded. This is similar to what my pastor meant when he compared integrity with stability because the less torn, we feel, the more centered, grounded and whole we feel and the more fragmented and torn we feel, the more unsure, uncertain and unstable we feel. In the book, *Remembering Wholeness,* Carol Tuttle shares that wholeness is not something we become, but rather something we remember. Her premise is that we are already whole and complete and it is our illusions which cause us to feel otherwise. Even though I am not yet at the place where I am convinced of my wholeness and completeness, I am also no longer feeling as ungrounded, uncentered and unstable as I used to feel. When I find myself feeling that way, I know that it is due to a sense of imbalance and then I remind myself that I am already whole and complete. I do this is through prayer, meditation, and grounding techniques. In the chapter on rest, I shared that one of my favorite grounding techniques is barefoot in the grass and connecting with the earth's energy. Whenever I do this, I begin to feel stable and centered within minutes. I also have clients who have equally found it to be very beneficial especially during times of emotional turmoil, anxiety, panic, stress and overwhelm. The truth is the more stable and grounded we are, the more we tend to operate more from our core self and less from our insecurities, doubts and fears. Also, the more stable and grounded we are, the more we can remain in the present and less in the past or the future. This is why mindfulness is so important because it helps us focus on the now and in essence feel more present and centered.

One of the greatest challenges I endured in my season of epiphany was in the area of my relationships when I started to notice certain changes with the people around me after I released my first book. It was subtle at first; not responding to text messages or returning phone calls, but eventually, it became quite obvious that certain people had no intention of supporting me on this leg of the journey. I remember thinking to myself that I was prepared for people outside of my circle to behave in certain ways, but I wasn't prepared to have that show up inside my inner circle. As much as I resisted it, my inner circle began to slowly transform and shrink. Now, I can see that God was removing things, people, habits and beliefs that were no longer suitable for where I was going, but at the time, I just remember feeling wounded. On the outside things were going great, but inside I was thinking, "If you only knew how much I have lost". I continued to pray and seek God for clarity and understanding as I questioned, "How can one of the most exciting times of my life also be the one of the worst times of my life?"

The following year, a funny thing happened. I started to accept the ending of those relationships and I slowly became comfortable being alone. I remembered having once read that the word alone is translated as "all one", meaning whole and complete. I also discovered that loneliness and aloneness are two different things, and that I could be alone without feeling lonely. Dr. Wayne Dyer states that we can never be lonely if we like who we are alone with, and I gradually started to like my own company. I realized and admitted to myself that I had been too dependent on other people to give me a sense of connectedness, belonging, validation and acceptance and I had been losing myself in the process. At this point, I intentionally began attending events by myself. It was also during this time that my mentor, Tobias, often reminded me that I was never "by" myself, I was always "with" myself. This simple shift in perspective helped me to stop feeling so abandoned.

I also started to connect with women who were on the same wavelength as me and I began to find my own tribe. It was then that I realized how letting go of relationships that were no longer meant to be in my life had opened doors to so many new opportunities! I stopped referring to those former relationships as a loss, because by losing them, I was finding me! For once, I became clear on what I truly wanted, expected and deserved in my relationships and I was no longer willing to settle for anything less. I set limits and boundaries with people and discovered the power of the word, "No", without guilt, apology or lengthy explanation. I started being invited into circles with people who were not threatened by me, people who congratulated and celebrated my success, and even offered to collaborate and assist me in my growth. Before long, those old hurts started to fade and I realized how much I had tolerated in my efforts to be liked and accepted.

Pursuing our dreams will cost us, but not pursuing them to try and hold onto someone or something will cost us even more. I remember hearing a speaker once say that "Heavy doesn't float" which means we cannot take everyone with us and we may have to get used to being alone. I finally stopped questioning God about why certain relationships ended and I started thanking Him for forcing me to demand and expect more for myself.

The truth is it takes courage to step out and pursue your own destiny. You will lose people and you will be judged, criticized, and ostracized by the very people from whom you seek support. You may have to get used to being alone, but you also may just learn to like and appreciate your own company. I never want to reach old age and spend my time regretting what I "coulda, shoulda, and woulda" done, if I had the courage to step out in faith and stand on my own even when I had to stand alone.

When I think back on that time in my life and how much I felt I had lost, I realize that I had not lost anything because every "loss" simply creates space for something new and better. I discovered the true meaning of this one day while deleting photos, videos, apps, and messages on my cellphone to free up some space. I noticed that when I finished, my phone did not show me how much I lost or the empty space I had left, it showed me what was now "available".

Personal Reflection:

1) What can you do to create more of a sense of wholeness within yourself?

2) Do you tend to find yourself stuck in the past or worrying about the future?

3) Do you have the courage to step out in pursuit of your divine purpose in life?

4) Are you afraid of what your success will cost? What is the cost of you not pursuing it?

Chapter 34

The Deep End

"When you go through deep waters, I will be with you"
~~Isaiah 43:2 NLT

In June of 2019, my husband and I rented an Air BnB for my daughter's sixth birthday party and sleepover. The location we chose was absolutely beautiful and came complete with a large in ground swimming pool that stretched from three to nine feet. My whole family came out to help us celebrate our little princess, including my barely two-year-old nephew, affectionately known as AJ. Little did I know that AJ and his mother - my sister - would teach me a valuable life lesson that day.

As my family and I sat around the pool deck, we watched with amusement as AJ continually inched closer and closer to the deep end of the pool. Several times my husband, who was standing close by, was able to derail his initial efforts to jump into the deep end, but eventually AJ seized his opportunity! While my family and I watched in horror, my two-year-old nephew stepped off the side of the pool right into nine feet of water! AJ, who had never taken a swim lesson and did not know how to swim, confidently slipped into the deep end of the pool wearing nothing but his arm floaties. My husband quickly reacted to try to get him out, but AJ showed absolutely no signs of fear, as he began laughing and playing right there in the deep end! I was shocked, but even more shocking was that his mother sat there calmly and did not react at all. I remember thinking to myself, "What is wrong with her?! Doesn't she see her baby in nine feet of water?" My sister then made a statement that shifted my entire perspective and changed the way I view so many things in life. She stated "He knows that if the floaties will keep him afloat in the shallow end, they will also keep him afloat in the deep end". Wow! I could not believe the simplicity of this statement, but I definitely understood the depth of it! As I reflected on it further, I began to wonder, "How many of us trust God, ourselves and the process in the shallow end but become afraid, doubtful, and untrusting in the deep end?

Eight years prior to this, I decided to learn to swim at the age of forty. I had never learned as a child and had always wanted to, so I signed up for lessons at the local YMCA and my sister, Tonya joined me. We both progressed well through the class and I could honestly say I learned to swim; that is, until it was time to go in the deep end! Our final test in the class involved swimming in the deep end with the kick board. I remember panicking as the realization of this sunk in and I understood what it meant. Not only would I have to swim in the deep end, I would have to leave behind the safety of the shallow end of the pool and go where my feet no longer touched the bottom. I would have to let go of the sense of control I had that if things went South, I could still save myself and exit the pool quickly. Helplessly, I stood and watched as my sister and another lady in our class navigated their way to the deep end of the pool for the swim test, but I could not bring myself to follow suit. I had spent the past few weeks learning to swim, hold my breath, dog paddle, tread water and even float, but I could not trust myself to let go of the safety of the shallow end. I knew enough to know that this wasn't just about swimming; this was a reflection of my inner fears of letting go, not being in control and trusting the process. Afterwards, I vowed to myself that I would sign up for lessons again and take the swim test in the deep end as I was determined to overcome this fear. I was determined to learn what it meant to approach the deep end fearlessly and trust myself to navigate it. I was determined to know what it would mean to totally surrender and trust God, even in the deep end. What my nephew and sister taught me that hot July day was not about swimming, but about faith, courage and trust. The same floaties that had kept my nephew afloat in the shallow end also kept him afloat in the deep end.

I have met many people who, like me, are afraid of the deep end. People who may be fine in the shallow end where there is a degree of control, predictability, and safety, but panic when life pulls them towards the deep end. I discovered that deep sea fishermen intentionally steer their boats to the deepest parts of the ocean because they know that is where they will discover and land the big fish. To do this, they must navigate far away from the shore, sometimes losing sight of it, where they cannot get out as quickly and their feet no longer touch the bottom. It's worth it to make the big catch. The same is true in life. The big wins, the big prizes, the big successes, the big deals, the big opportunities, the big money and the big risk are all in the deep end, and only those with the right amount of determination, faith, courage, willingness or just plain fearlessness will go out that far to get it.

I have shared this story on numerous occasions as inspiration to people who are going after the big fish in life, because no matter what our dreams are or how big they appear to be, the God who is with us in the shallow end is the same God who will be with us in the deep end. And if you're going to dream anyway, you might as well go big!

Personal Reflection:

1) What are you hoping for and striving for that seems too big, too far, or too grand?

2) Are you playing it safe in the shallow end?

3) What are you willing to do to get the big wins?

Chapter 35

Look Again: Change Your Perspective

"If you change the way you look at things,
the things you look at change"
~~Dr. Wayne Dyer

"Look Again" came to me after I finished hosting my second women's conference only to realize that I had lost money on yet another "successful" event. Following the success of my first event where I had made a profit, I decided to go with a larger venue across town. I had speakers fly in from across the country and even a world-famous celebrity Pastor as my featured speaker. The décor was beautiful, the food was great, the opening performance was incredible, the event was well planned and executed, and people were praising me and my team on the success of the event and even suggesting we take it on tour.

The financial projections I made prior to the event indicated a huge profit; however, when I received the final invoice from the venue, I realized that not only had I not made a profit, I was actually short. Immediately, I felt aggravated, frustrated and disappointed and I began to question the point of it.

As I was searching for meaning and understanding, I began sharing my thoughts and feelings with my friend, LaDonya. She made a statement that stopped me still in my tracks and shifted my entire perspective. She said, "It wasn't a failure even if it looks and feels that way. Look again, my friend." It was so simplistic and yet extremely profound and instantly I was reminded of two stories in the Bible. One was in the Book of Kings when the prophet Elijah, who had been praying and expecting rain, sent his servant to look for evidence of it. Six times, the servant was instructed to go up and look for rain, and each time came back saying he had seen nothing. I can imagine Elijah saying "Look Again" as he instructed his servant to go back a seventh time. This time, however, the servant came back and reported seeing a cloud in the distance no bigger than the size of a man's hand. At that point, Elijah advised Ahab to prepare for a heavy rain and soon after, the heavy rains came. The second story that came to mind is in the Book of John when Jesus healed a blind man by spitting on his eyes. Afterwards, Jesus asked the man if he could see anything and the man replied he saw people that looked like trees walking. Jesus then laid his hands on the man's eyes again and the man's vision was perfectly restored. Once again, I can imagine Jesus saying "Look Again".

"Look again" is being able to see beyond our physical sight because things are not always as they appear. It means focusing on our accomplishments rather than our apparent failures. It means intentionally seeing the good even when our eyes may be perceiving something else. When my friend advised me to look again, I began to understand that I could choose to continue to look at the event as a failure because it had not earned a profit, or I could look beyond the obvious and gain a fresh new perspective. Once I was able to shift my perspective, I realized that my event had been a success and I would not allow the lack of financial gain to determine or define that success. My event was the first women's conference hosted by a woman of color at this venue and the room was filled with women from across the United States. Secondly, women were calling it the best women's conference they had ever attended and celebrity Pastor, John Gray, showed up and took photos with everyone. Most importantly, women's lives were touched in a whole new way and the testimonials we received afterwards were mind-blowing!

Perspective is defined as a way of viewing something and I often have to assist my clients with shifting the way they have been viewing or replaying some troublesome life event. By shifting their perspectives, they are able to look at things in a way that may be instrumental in helping them release their inner feelings of blame, shame, guilt, anger and resentment. Shifting our perspectives is not about denying something that happened or whitewashing it, it is about simply choosing to look at it a different way so that we are able to choose how we identify it and what it means to us. Oftentimes, we struggle because of the definitions and meaning we have assigned to certain events in our lives. For example, someone who was dumped by a lover may realize that they were settling, and they now have the opportunity to meet the man or woman of their dreams. A person who loses a job may recognize it as an opportunity to start the business they have been putting off for years. I can honestly say that although Covid-19 has certainly changed life as we know it, some of the benefits for me and my family have been that we have gotten more rest and had a chance to slow down and reconnect. It is all in how we choose to view things.

I once had a client whose husband had been injured on the job and was no longer able to return to his previous line of work. As a result, he had slipped into a deep depression because he had lost his sizeable income and their family had to downsize their home and give up a lot of luxuries to which they had grown accustomed. One day when he brought his wife to her session, he mentioned this to me. After validating his experience and assuring him that I understood what he and his family had lost, I asked him one simple question, "What do you have left?" He paused to consider this and told me he would get back to me. A few weeks later when he brought his wife to her next appointment, he walked into my lobby, smiling, and proceeded to lift me off my feet (he was about 6'7") and spin me in the air. I was confused and caught off guard until he explained that he had been thinking about my question and it finally hit him that while he could no longer work his old job, he now had the freedom to pursue projects that he had always wanted to pursue and wasn't able to, because of his work schedule and financial commitments. He also stated that he missed working with his hands and had begun creating things again. As a result, he and his wife had started a home-based business and were making money selling things from their front lawn. After putting me down, he thanked me and with tears in his eyes, he told me that my question had singlehandedly changed his life and his depression had begun to go away.

Another example of Look Again came to me as we approached our second Thanksgiving holiday without my mother. I was feeling down because my siblings and I were not spending Thanksgiving Day together. My younger sister had to work, my older sister had decided to eat dinner at a friend's house, and my in-laws were either working or had other plans as well. That meant it would just be my husband, my children and myself. Growing up, holidays were always a big production at our house and I could only think of one Thanksgiving where I was not at home in my entire 47 years of life. Needless to say, I was not only missing my mother, I was also dreading a quiet holiday without my family. Even my son asked me, "Mommy, is it going to be just us?" I stayed in a funk for weeks until one day I heard God say to me, "If you will let go of what has to be, I can show you what can be". Stunned, I continued listening for more understanding. God then reminded me of how I had always wanted to go to a cabin in the mountains or visit NYC and see the Macy's Thanksgiving Day parade, but had never been able to because of my family commitment. I began to feel a lightness as my mind started to conceive all the things, we could now do to celebrate the holiday in "a new way". I thought of taking the children to Disney World or Paradise Island in The Bahamas and I became excited. I then began thinking of creative ideas for our family to spend our first Thanksgiving alone with "just us". My husband and I cooked a big meal and we all put on our pajamas and made S'mores outside by the firepit while we shared what we were grateful for. The evening ended with my husband reading Christmas stories. That evening, my son said to me, "Mommy, this was the best day ever!" This simple lesson has taught me the power and the value of being able to change our perspective and focus on the gifts that are inherent in all of our life lessons, both the successes and the perceived failures. To top it off, my family and I got the chance to spend Thanksgiving 2019 in NYC in the middle of Times Square two blocks from the Macy's parade route. It was truly the experience of a lifetime!

I still have to remind myself at times to change my perspective and remember to count my blessings when I get disappointed or discouraged because things did not work out as planned. I remind myself to look for the gift within the situation; remember what I have left; let go of how something has to be, used to be or should be, so I can discover the infinite possibilities of what can be.

Suffering is Optional

I was sitting in the middle of a session with a client one day, when I had an aha moment in regards to the Buddhist quote, "Pain is inevitable, suffering is optional." I listened as she shared her story of pain and suffering when it hit me: "Pain will happen to us at some point and we cannot avoid or escape it. Suffering, however, is optional". By definition, pain is a physical or emotional sensation in the body that tells us something is happening; suffering is the interpretation, belief, and judgment we make about what is happening. In essence, it is our story, the narrative. The reality is that at some point, we will all experience physical and emotional pain; from physical injury, disease, and discomfort, to emotional pain such as disappointment, anger, depression and sadness. We cannot control or predict everything we are going to experience in this life, but we can control how we respond to it. We can choose when to suffer, how to suffer or whether or not we will suffer at all. Often, we end up stuck and unable to move forward after unfortunate events in life because it's almost as if we have some need to suffer. I have seen this play out many times with clients who are interpreting events from their past that are actually contributing to their pain and suffering! For example, a person who felt rejected by a parent may interpret that to mean they are unlovable or not good enough. This story of not may follow them throughout their entire lives and cause years of unnecessary suffering. The reality is that a parent who rejects you reveals absolutely nothing about you and everything about themselves. Likewise, a relationship ending may mean it was time for us to move on because we have outgrown it, rather than it being an indication that we will end up alone. What we tell ourselves - our stories, become what we live by and one of the greatest sources of our pain and suffering. If our story tells us we are loved and valued, then we will live our lives in that way and engage in relationships with that belief and expectation. If our story tells us we are unwanted and inferior, unless we do the work to overcome those beliefs, we will see evidence of it play out in every arena of our lives.

I used to believe that suffering was a natural part of life and the only way for us to learn our lessons. I bought into that belief and as you can probably guess, that is exactly what I experienced time and time again. Instead of examining why, I kept asking myself what I was doing wrong when the real question was what I was believing. I finally realized that not all of our life lessons have to be learned the hard way, and that it is quite possible for us to learn our lessons in love. When we understand that life is for us, the lessons become blessings in disguise, challenges become opportunities and setbacks become setups for us to win. Unfortunately, most of us have been conditioned to only make changes in response to pain or discomfort. For example, we only pay attention to our health when there is an illness we must face, and we only pursue our dreams when our jobs are taken away.

I can remember learning this valuable lesson when I quit my job of nine years to go into private practice. Everyone around me was questioning why I would leave such a "good job" to start my own business. While I understood their logic, I also knew it was time for me to move on. This was when I realized that most of us have a fear of letting go of something good for something great, and will only give ourselves permission to pursue what we truly desire in life when the "good job" ends or the comfortable situation is no longer comfortable. Otherwise, we feel risky, foolish and afraid to break the rules. Instead, we wait until we are forced to make a change instead of choosing to make a change, which makes us reactors as opposed to creators. Some of our lessons will include a certain amount of pain and others may come with indescribable pain because unfortunately, sometimes this is the only way for life to wake us up to a realization and understanding about something we have been ignoring and avoiding.

Two years ago, I started taking Tuesdays off as my "personal retreat day". I would spend the entire day with no TV, no social media, no meetings or even lunch with friends; just a full day-of-silence and solitude for me with me. In the beginning, I worried that I would get less done by taking off a whole day to do nothing, but what I discovered was that I actually became more productive on the other days I worked. My day off to rest and recharge gave me new energy and reinvigorated my passion for what I do. While I understand not everyone has the luxury to take off an extra day due to their work schedule, the point is that even though I always had the choice to do it, I had never made the decision to do it until I started to experience fatigue. Why do we ignore life's little taps on the shoulder until we are hit in the head with a brick? I can honestly admit that I was notorious for that, notorious for ignoring my own needs and priorities so I could be there for other people, and notorious for tuning out the wisdom of my own inner voice to listen to someone else's opinions, ideas and problems. I have since changed all of that and I now make time to listen and take heed before life hits me over the head to get my attention. I won't always get it right and neither will you. We will learn some of our lessons through the presence and experience of pain, but even then, we still get to choose whether to suffer. We still get to decide what it means and how we are going to respond. As Charles Swindoll says, "Life is 10% of what happens to us and 90% of how we respond to it" which means that you and I can choose whether life is full of misery, pain and suffering, or if our painful events are really opportunities to grow. We may not always be able to control the events or avoid the pain, but we can always control the narrative and choose to suffer or not.

Personal Reflection:

1) Is there an area of your life where you need to Look Again and change your perspective?

2) Have you suffered a loss of some kind and need to refocus on what you have left?

3) Have you been choosing to suffer as a result of painful experiences?

4) What if you change how you interpreted those events? Would the story change?

5) What challenges are you currently facing that could be viewed as opportunities?

Chapter 36

Fear Not

"Be afraid, and do it anyway"
~~Unknown

Perhaps one of the greatest epiphanies and lessons I learned during my journey has been in regards to fear. Fear is a dreaded word to many and a majority of people can admit to struggling with fear and wondering how to manage and overcome it. I too have struggled with enormous amounts of fear in many aspects of my life. Growing up, I was afraid of bees. No, let me correct that. I was afraid of anything that crawled or flew. While summers were a fun time, they were also a dreaded period for me because I grew up during a time when there were no video games or other reasons to stay indoors. I was also raised in a household with a mother who believed children should be outside playing, and because we did not have central air conditioning, playing outside was preferable to being inside. And because I grew up in a rural town, there were many "adventures" for young children to venture into and my siblings and cousins frequently challenged each other to conquer some new feat of bravery. Looking back on some of those challenges, I wonder how we all managed to escape childhood without more broken bones, bruises, dog bites, etc. While I desperately wanted to fit in and prove myself, many of the things we did scared me to no end. I was afraid of heights, afraid of insects, afraid of the dark, afraid of being alone, afraid of authority figures, afraid of being teased and afraid of being left out. It is safe to say that fear played a major role in my life throughout my childhood. Just like many of us, I thought fear was either something to overcome or avoid altogether. I never knew then that fear had a purpose or could serve a purpose. All I knew was that fear caused my heart rate to increase, palms to sweat, and breathing to change, if I even remembered to breathe.

In my early adulthood, fear continued to play a major role in my life, but it took on different forms. While I was no longer as afraid of all insects, and I no longer feared being by myself, I still struggled with fears of being left out and fears of being criticized and rejected. Add to that, new fears such as not having enough money, not finding a career I loved, not getting married and having children, not succeeding in life, not knowing my purpose, and fear of never overcoming my childhood wounds. Rather than confront my fears in an intentional manner, I did like many people do, I buried them, denied them, avoided them, rationalized them, and hid them. Eventually some of my fears were alleviated when I bought my first home, built and sold another home, finished graduate school and earned my Master's degree in Counseling and landed a job I really liked. I went on to meet and marry my husband, and I gave birth to my son and daughter. On the outside, my life was becoming more stable and secure, but fear was always there just beneath the surface. The fears I had already accumulated in my life combined with the fear of my husband leaving me, fear of not being a good parent, fear of leaving my job to start my private counseling practice, and so on. I can still remember almost having a panic attack the day my first book was completed and my husband uploaded it for publishing. My new fears were, "What if no one likes the book? What if no one buys it? What if I am really not a good writer? What if people judge me or look at me differently now that they know the truth behind my mask?" Reflecting back, it was a weird place to be: on one hand, the things I had longed for were happening and on the other hand, I was feeling resistant and afraid. Determined not to quit, I remembered the commitment I had made to myself a year prior to that, which was if I did not reach my full God-given potential, it would not be because of me. It would not be because of my fears of people, the unknown, change, growth, attention, scrutiny, rejection, or anything else. I committed to do my inner work and face and overcome whatever I had to in order to allow myself every opportunity to embody the full extent of my experience. I became willing to do things afraid and not let fear stop me, and it was during some of my darkest hours, when I was consumed with the most amount and intensity of fear that my relationship with fear began to shift. I was praying to God one day and asking Him to help me overcome my fears in the hopes that I would no longer feel them and would be free to move forward and face things more courageously. All of a sudden, something in me shifted and a dawning of discovery, realization and awakening occurred almost instantaneously. It was like the clouds inside my mind dissipated and I could see with crystal clear clarity and understanding. I heard myself say aloud, "Fear is not my enemy nor my adversary. Fear is simply my internal warning system". I realized then that fear is meant to warn us of real danger and it activates our body's fight, flight, freeze response. It even does this without me having to consciously think about it. It simply reacts. In that exact moment, I understood that fear was not trying to harm me or hold me back, it was actually doing what is had been designed to do, protect me. Its purpose is to help me survive and stay alive.

My second discovery was that fear is an indicator. It indicates areas in my life where I am not yet healed or evolved. For example, my fear of being exposed was really rooted in my fear of people finding out I was not good enough. So, if I could do the work to clear this limiting belief, that fear would no longer exist because it would no longer serve a purpose. My fear of being alone indicated that I did not feel whole within myself and needed other people to fulfill and complete me. My fear of rejection was rooted in my fears of not being accepted and I realized that once I learned to fully and unconditionally accept me, I would no longer need anyone else's acceptance or fear the lack of their acceptance. After that, I began to view fear in a whole different light and it became something I no longer needed to avoid, deny, run from or bury. I knew I could now begin to face the things I feared, discover the messages within those things, and learn the necessary lessons to heal and grow. With this epiphany and awakening, I understood that our objective to overcome fear and remove fear is somewhat misguided. Our objective should be to face our fears, search within them for meaning and understanding, or simply acknowledge them and thank them for assisting us on our journeys. This does not mean we will no longer have any fears. I am still having to face and address some areas of fear and every time I do; I evolve and grow to a whole new level. I remember once reading that there are only two emotions and those are love and fear. In the book, *Mirror Work*, Author Louise Hay says that "Fear is a lack of love and trust in ourselves, life and the world around us" which brings to mind the scripture that says "perfect love casteth out fear". As you and I continue to grow in love and trust in ourselves, our fears will no longer feel the need to protect us from everything in order to prevent us from injury. Fear will simply become what it was intended to be when our ancestors were facing real dangers that threatened their survival.

In truth, our fears can be real or imaginary and our minds do not know the difference. I often assist my clients in identifying rational fears - such as an escaped lion - and irrational fears. As a therapist, I have met numerous people struggling with a variety of fears that feel and appear to be rational, but are often rooted in something deeper. There is a direct connection between fear, stress and worry on our mental and emotional health as well as negative impacts on our physical health. There are even studies that show that stress and worry lead to premature aging and weight gain. Whenever our parasympathetic nervous system is activated in fight, flight or freeze mode, our bodies release the hormone cortisol which fuels our adrenaline and activates all of our internal systems to prepare us to fight, flee or freeze. When the danger passes or the stressor is removed, the body is supposed to return to a natural resting state. However, because many of us remain in danger mode, panic mode, survival mode, and crisis mode, the body is never able to return to a resting state and cortisol is continuously released into the blood stream causing weight gain and other issues within the body.

If we can begin to shift our relationship with fear, we can accept that fear is our internal warning system and while feeling afraid at times is a natural response, living in fear is anything but natural, which is why it bothers us and causes us so much distress. Once we recognize this, we can stop seeing fear as an adversary to be avoided and resisted, which will allow us to discover the messages within our fears and do the work that is necessary live happier, healthier lives.

Personal Reflection:

1) How would your life be different if you had a new relationship with fear?

2) How would you show up differently?

3) What would change if you no longer allowed fear to hold you back?

Chapter 37

Locked from the Inside

"Why do you stay in prison
when the door is so wide open"
~~Rumi

We have never lived in a time where we have been so conscious and had access to as much knowledge, wisdom, insight and freedom of choice as we do now. I understand that there are many people who would disagree with me because their personal experiences are in direct contradiction of this; because the reality is that we have also never lived in a time when there has been so much racial division, hatred, mass shootings, suicide, depression, bullying, global health crises, and everything else from modern day slavery and human trafficking to ongoing terrorist threats and attacks. The world currently feels more like Hell on earth rather than a happy, peaceful place, and certainly nothing like Heaven.

One afternoon, I was watching a docuseries on Netflix and Neale Donald Walsh, author of *Conversations with God*, mentioned a quote "The gates of hell are locked from the inside". Of course, this fascinated me. Being a lover of psychology and philosophy and working with clients who regularly feel as if they are imprisoned mentally and emotionally and I understand people feeling like they are locked in Hell. I have even had clients describe experiences of seeing themselves locked away in a castle, dungeon or underground tunnel. One of the most amazing things for me to witness is when someone discovers that this is only an illusion and that they have had access to leave the entire time. It is a wonderful demonstration of epiphany.

Interestingly, I too once felt stuck, trapped, locked away and imprisoned, waiting for God or someone else to come along and rescue me. It was during therapy that I discovered that my worst enemy was actually me and the thoughts, beliefs, memories, and feelings, that were keeping me trapped and imprisoned; therefore, I was locking the gates of my own private Hell from the inside and there was no gatekeeper. I went on to discover that while it was true, I had been abused and victimized, the reality was that none of those things were happening to me in the present. But because I was still "mentally bound", I continued to feel helpless, powerless and imprisoned and every time I attempted to really step out and pursue my dreams, something would always seem to pull me back. I called it fear, and even though it was fear, I realized it was of my own mental creation and not some boogeyman waiting to punish me for daring to be happy, healthy and whole. As I continued to do my inner work and overcome the effects of my past, I began to see myself in a whole different light. I stopped feeling trapped and I started to feel of liberated and free. Ironically, this initially scared me too. I assume it's similar to how some prisoners feel when they are released and find that they are still afraid to use the restroom without asking for permission. They are free on the outside, but not on the inside. I realized I no longer wanted to be my own worst enemy or any kind of enemy to me, and I no longer wanted to hold myself back or punish myself for some perceived wrongdoing. I longed to live free and I longed to lead my clients and other people to freedom. I wanted to feel and experience freedom from fear, insecurities, self-judgment, and self-criticism and unforgiveness. I wanted to be free to laugh and relax and just be. I wanted to be free to open up and let my guard down and invite people in. When my brother, Tommy was incarcerated for a period of time, I remember seeing a book he had been reading entitled, *Free on the Inside*. At the time, I figured it meant feeling free while being locked inside of prison, but I now believe it also meant feeling free on the inside of us. Out of the heart flow the issues of life, so if we feel trapped, stuck and imprisoned inside, it really does not matter how much external freedom we have or how many rights to freedom, we will hold ourselves back, prevent ourselves from moving forward, become our own worst enemies and live a life of limitation and restriction. In essence, we will lock the gates from the inside.

Freedom is defined as the power or right to act, speak and think as one wants without hindrance or restraint. While I know this is not always guaranteed, especially among minorities and other disenfranchised people, it is still the definition of the freedoms we have been promised, even if they are not always upheld. In the beginning of this chapter, I stated that we have never lived in a time when we have been so conscious or had "access" to so much freedom, and I still stand by that regardless of what I sometimes witness in the media or in my own community. I am determined to live free, to think freely and teach my children these same ideals. As someone who has lived much of her life locked inside her own mental prison, I am determined not to live one more minute denying, restricting or resisting my freedom. My life may not become heaven on earth, but it doesn't have to be hell on earth either, and if I am going to be imprisoned, it certainly will not be of my own doing. Living free for me means being free to be happy, healthy and whole. Free to choose where to live, what type of work I do, how much money I earn where my children attend school and what to buy and cook for dinner.

Even though minorities living in America or other countries of the world may not always have our freedoms guaranteed or upheld, we can always choose what and how to think and we can always choose to live free on the inside.

Personal Reflection:

1) Do you feel free? If the answer is no, is it of your own doing? Is it the result of past experiences or mental conditioning? Are you your own worst enemy?

2) What are you willing to do to live free?

3) When was the last time you felt free? Describe the feeling.

4) If you are trapped in a situation such as an abusive relationship or even a job you hate, how can you begin to feel free on the inside?

Chapter 38

You Can Have It All

"You are your only limit"
~~Unknown

Most likely, you have heard two different messages when it comes to having it all: one being that you can have it all. You can have good health, a great marriage or relationship, successful happy children, financial abundance, spiritual and emotional freedom, and physical health and well-being. On the other hand, you may have heard that no one has it all and everyone is missing something or struggling to overcome some issue. You may have been told that the key is in being okay with not having it all and being grateful for what you do have…because no one has it all. I have heard the same messages and while I probably thought the message saying I can have it all was a bit far-fetched or a great sales pitch for some new success coach or financial guru, I knew that inside of me, I wanted it all. Not all as in an amount per se…not all the happiness in the world, or all the money, or all the good breaks or all the success, but when I was honest with myself, I realized I did want it all. I did want a healthy body, a happy marriage, successful happy children, financial abundance and a great life of happiness, friendship, love and well-being. I thought to myself, "Don't we all secretly long for that? Who is honestly saying I am just grateful for being rich and it doesn't matter if I am sick or my family is a mess? Who is saying, I might be physically healthy, but I am okay with no friends or loved ones to spend my time with or money to enjoy life with?" Isn't part of the purpose in this journey called life about having it all? Isn't this what Jesus meant by having life and having it more abundantly? Or was I the only one who was confused and misinformed? Was it just me who wanted it all and would probably spend my entire life striving to have it all and never actually reach it because having it all is impossible? One of the most beautiful things about writing this book is not only the amazing lessons I have learned and the messages I feel were downloaded directly from God, but also the incredible amount of wisdom and knowledge I have gained from others. This journey, this epiphany season, has taken me back to many books I have read over the years and introduced me to works I had never heard of such as *The Big Leap* by Gay Hendrix, *The Power* by Rhonda Byrne, *The Magic* by Rhonda Byrne, *The Four Agreements* by Don Miguel Ruiz, and so many others; however, it was the book, *You'll See it When You Believe it*, by Dr. Wayne Dyer that truly educated me about having it all. Dr. Dyer said that we *can* have it all because we *are* it all. Already. It was so simple and yet so profound at the same time. Once again, I had forgotten the entire message contained in this book. It is not about getting, achieving, having, buying or even doing. It is about being. I, you, we can have it all when we realize, embrace and understand that we are it all, that we are missing and lacking nothing and that we are not incomplete or inadequate. Having it all does not make us more whole, more complete or more of anything. We came here complete…with no possessions, titles, or achievements other than breathing. Having it all is being it all; being happy, being successful, being healthy, being at peace, being enough, being whole, and being perfect just as we are right where we are. Sure, we can have the stuff, but let's always be reminded that the stuff does not make us, define us, or complete us. It is just stuff, and we cannot take any of it with us. We came here with nothing and were at once, whole, perfect and complete and we will leave here with nothing, whole, perfect and complete. The stuff is temporary; we are eternal.

In several chapters of this book, I have written about my work with low wealth clients and millionaire clients and found the same common theme. Money, success, achievement, and stuff does not guarantee happiness, peace, fulfillment or wholeness. Those things are the icing on the cake, the overflow of goodness, but not the source of the good or the supply of it. I have watched rich people and poor people struggle to overcome not feeling adequate or good enough by buying more stuff, having more things, traveling more places, having more relationships or achieving more goals, and while these things certainly may bring a degree of satisfaction, excitement and even joy, inevitably they end up needing more to stay filled up. Again, we live in the land of opportunity with every conceivable and available resource, yet we are growing more and more depressed, anxious and suicidal as a nation using food, drugs, alcohol, sex, and a host of other vices to self-medicate and numb ourselves. You are it all. I am it all. We are a part of it all. One of the definitions for the word "all" is whole, and wholeness is not what we get, accomplish or become, it is who we are. Perhaps this is the greatest epiphany of all for me…discovering and accepting that I am already whole, perfect and complete even as I continue my journey of learning, laughing, living, and loving. And so are you.

Personal Reflection:

1) What does having it all mean to you?

2) Now that you understand you are it all already, how does this shift things?

Chapter 39

Full Circle: Coming Home to Yourself

"It was when I stopped searching for home within others, and lifted
the foundations of home within myself, I found there were
no roots more intimate than those between a
mind and body that have decided to be whole"
~~Rupi Kaur

If I could adequately sum up my journey of self-discovery, awakening, awareness, growth, revelation and enlightenment, I would say my greatest understanding is that this whole experience has not only been about me coming full circle, but rather me coming home to myself. Coming full circle means completing a cycle and returning to the beginning, and although I am returning to my true, authentic self, I realize that once the mind is stretched in a new direction, it won't ever go back to the exact same, so my journey has really been about coming home. To come home to oneself basically means to discover yourself, outside of other people's opinions and ideas about you and outside of your many roles and responsibilities. It means being stripped bare of all your external attributes and realizing that the *you* reflecting back at you in the mirror is at once incredible, amazing, perfect, whole and complete. Even more so is understanding that you have never been anything other than that.

Coming home to yourself is when you are no longer searching for yourself within your relationships, possessions or accomplishments. It is when you realize that every experience in your life, good and bad, has been leading up to this very moment and this very moment is the only one that matters. It is when you are beyond the need for external acceptance, approval, validation, consent, permission, or praise because you are willing and committed to giving those things to yourself first! Coming home is when you recognize that home is not a place, a building, a city, an environment, a marriage, a status or a house, home is an inner knowing that nothing outside of you has the power to define you and determine your destiny. Coming home is when you intuitively know that you belong and that you have always had a seat at the table. It is when you know you are wanted, necessary and essential, without anyone having to invite you or include you. It is when you understand and accept that you are worthy of health and wealth, happiness and well-being, and greatness and success. It is when you are your own best friend and the biggest source of support you will ever need. It is when you realize that wealth and abundance is your birthright and not a privilege or a pipe dream. Coming home is when you know without a doubt that you are loved, accepted and good enough just as you are, because you are, and you carry this truth within you everywhere you go. Coming home is having faith in yourself and in your innate ability to confront whatever comes your way. It is when you trust yourself and give yourself permission to venture out into the deep end because you know that God is with you and will never leave nor forsake you. It is when you realize that beauty is not only what you see, it is how you see it and you are willing to recognize your own internal and external beauty without guilt, shame or apology. As a result, you are also able to see the beauty in everyone and everything else. Coming home is when you no longer fear the unknown and the unseen, and you trust yourself and you trust God. It is when you have the courage to stand up, speak out and make your voice heard. It is when you come out of hiding and no longer have a fear of being seen. Coming home is when you shift your relationship with fear and realize that it is an indicator of how you are still growing and warning for real and actual danger. It is when you forgive all the emotional debts you have been holding against other people and you also cancel the debts you are holding against yourself. It is when you overcome and resolve feelings of guilt, blame and shame and begin living freely from the inside out. Coming home is when you are no longer afraid to ask for what you want and deserve, and you do so boldly and expectantly. It is when you are open to receive that which you have asked for, and you become a conduit and a channel for your blessings to flow unimpededly. It is when you are in alignment with yourself and what you desire in life. It is when you no longer have need to struggle and swim upstream to prove yourself to anyone for any reason. It is when you stop holding back, shrinking, fading, or dimming your light for fear of outshining anyone and everyone around you. It is when you feel safe, secure and protected and realize that you are not small, helpless or powerless. You can walk and speak with courage knowing that any battle that is too big for you to win, God will fight and win for you. Coming home to yourself is when you can give grace and mercy to yourself and you discover how easy it is to also give it to others. It is when you realize that you never had to be perfect to be loved, accepted or good enough and that all you ever had to do was show up and "be". It is when you can sit in silence with yourself, breathing freely and deeply as you embrace all that life still has to offer you. Coming home is when you know that your holding patterns and waiting rooms are just temporary states of being and that you can trust God and the Law of Gestation to bring about everything in divine timing. It is when you know that as within so without, and your external experiences are mere reflections of your internal being. It is knowing that everything is energy and has a vibration, a frequency, and a rhythm. Home is when you are no longer willing to play it safe and stay in the comfort zone, because you know that the possibility zone is where the magic happens. Home is when you can look in the mirror and instead of criticizing every flaw and imperfection, you smile as you witness the absolute miracle of your very being. Coming home is when you understand that we were never meant to control or predict life, but to surrender and trust the process. It is when you realize that you can care without carrying the burdens of others. Finally, coming home is when you have looked high and low, near and far for heroes and masters only to discover that the Kingdom of Heaven is within and that God is always alive in you, as you, and through you.

It has taken me two full years to finish writing Epiphany and as I complete this final chapter, I am filled with a myriad of emotions. I realize that a part of me was afraid to finish this book for fear that it would mean the end of my journey, when really this is only the beginning. Like the caterpillar going through its transformation and becoming a creature unrecognizable even to itself, I now know that I have embarked on a journey that will be perpetually unfolding and never-ending. As I reflect on all that has happened in the past few years, I am filled with immense joy and gratitude that God has been so incredibly present throughout this entire journey and has urged me to see myself as He sees me and love and myself unconditionally. I am also grateful for the woman I am and the woman I am becoming for having the courage to stay the course and finish this work when all I wanted to do sometimes was give up and give in, and I am grateful to "Little G" for being patient as I did the work to overcome my past and become healthy and whole again as we remember who we are and awaken the sleeping giant within.

While this journey has been painful and difficult, it has also been worth it; and if I had to relive every experience that brought me here, I would gladly do it again, for I have found that life is indeed a classroom and our experiences and the people we encounter are our teachers. When we get out of our own way and recognize that there really are no villains and we are not victims, we will see that everything really is for our good in the end. Every person who has ever rejected me forced me to accept myself; every person who ever betrayed me taught me to never betray myself; every person who ever abandoned me forced me to find peace within myself; every person who lied or deceived me taught me to always be true to myself; and every person who ever hurt me taught me that I am not my experiences and my experiences do not define me. I can truly see how God has used every painful situation to heal, educate, enlighten and liberate me as I use those experiences to help heal and liberate others. I thank Him for that and I thank you for sharing this journey with me.

My sincere hope is that you will discover your own inner truths and come home to yourself, where you too will discover a peace that surpasses all understanding and a sanctuary that feels like you never left. As you continue on your journey, keep in mind that it means absolutely nothing for you to win externally if you're losing internally. As the Bible says, "What does it profit a man (or woman) to gain the whole world and lose his soul?" I encourage you to do the work, play hard and win from the inside out!

Until we meet again…

www.ingramcontent.com/pod-product-compliance
Lightning Source LLC
Chambersburg PA
CBHW060013100426
42740CB00010B/1478